The Faithful Shepherdess

John Fletcher

To my Friend Master JOHN FLETCHER *upon his Faithfull Shepherdess.*

I know too well, that, no more than the man
That travels through the burning Desarts, can
When he is beaten with the raging Sun,
Half smothered in the dust, have power to run
From a cool River, which himself doth find,
E're he be slacked; no more can he whose mind
Joyes in the Muses, hold from that delight,
When nature, and his full thoughts bid him write:
Yet wish I those whom I for friends have known,
To sing their thoughts to no ears but their own.
Why should the man, whose wit ne'r had a stain,
Upon the publick Stage present his [vein,]
And make a thousand men in judgment sit,
To call in question his undoubted wit,
Scarce two of which can understand the laws
Which they should judge by, nor the parties cause?
Among the rout there is not one that hath
In his own censure an explicite faith;
One company knowing they judgement lack,
Ground their belief on the next man in black:
Others, on him that makes signs, and is mute,
Some like as he does in the fairest sute,
He as his Mistress doth, and she by chance:
Nor want there those, who as the Boy doth dance
Between the Acts, will censure the whole Play;
Some if the Wax-lights be not new that day;
But multitudes there are whose judgement goes
Headlong according to the Actors cloathes.
For this, these publick things and I, agree
So ill, that but to do a right for thee,
I had not been perswaded to have hurl'd
These few, ill spoken lines, into the world,
Both to be read, and censur'd of, by those,
Whose very reading makes Verse senseless Prose:
Such as must spend above an hour, to spell
A Challenge on a Past, to know it well:
But since it was thy hap to throw away
Much wit, for which the people did not pay,
Because they saw it not, I not dislike
This second publication, which may strike

Their consciences, to see the thing they scorn'd,
To be with so much wit and Art adorned.
Besides one vantage more in this I see,
Tour censurers now must have the qualitie
Of reading, which I am afraid is more
Than half your shrewdest Judges had before.

Fr. Beaumont.

To the worthy Author M'r. Jo. FLETCHER.

The wise, and many headed Bench, *that sits*
Upon the Life, and Death of Playes, *and* Wits,
(Composed of Gamester, Captain, Knight, Knight's man,
Lady, *or* Pusill, *that wears mask or fan,*
Velvet, *or* Taffata *cap, rank'd in the dark*
With the shops Foreman, *or some such* brave spark,
That may judge for his six-pence*) had, before*
They saw it half, damn'd thy whole Play, and more,
Their motives were, since it had not to doe
With vices, which they look'd for, and came to.

I, that am glad, thy Innocence was thy Guilt,
And wish that all the Muses *blood were spilt*
In such a Martyrdome, *to vex their eyes,*
Do crown thy murdred Poeme: *which shall rise*
A glorified work to Time, when Fire,
Or mothes shall eat, what all these Fools admire.

BEN. JONSON.

This Dialogue newly added, was spoken by way of Prologue to both
their Majesties, at the first acting of this Pastoral at *Somerset-house* on
Twelfth-night, 1633.

Priest.

A broiling Lamb on Pans *chief Altar lies,*
My Wreath, my Censor, Virge, and Incense by:
But I delayed the pretious Sacrifice,
To shew thee here, a Gentle Deity.

Nymph.

Nor was I to thy sacred Summons slow,
Hither I came as swift as th' Eagles wing,
Or threatning shaft from vext Dianaes *bow,*
To see this Islands God; the worlds best King.

Priest.

Bless then that Queen, that doth his eyes invite
And ears, t'obey her Scepter, half this night.

Nymph.

Let's sing such welcomes, as shall make Her sway
Seem easie to Him, though it last till day.

Welcom as Peace t'unwalled Cities, when
Famine and Sword leave them more graves than men.
As Spring to Birds, or Noon-dayes Sun to th' old
Poor mountain Muscovite congeal'd with cold.
As Shore toth' Pilot in a safe known Coast
When's Card is broken and his Rudder lost.

The Faithful Shepherdess

Actus Primus. Scena Prima.

Enter Clorin *a shepherdess, having buried her Love in an Arbour.*

Hail, holy Earth, whose cold Arms do imbrace
The truest man that ever fed his flocks
By the fat plains of fruitful *Thessaly*,
Thus I salute thy Grave, thus do I pay
My early vows, and tribute of mine eyes
To thy still loved ashes; thus I free
My self from all insuing heats and fires
Of love: all sports, delights and jolly games
That Shepherds hold full dear, thus put I off.
Now no more shall these smooth brows be begirt
With youthful Coronals, and lead the Dance;
No more the company of fresh fair Maids
And wanton Shepherds be to me delightful,
Nor the shrill pleasing sound of merry pipes
Under some shady dell, when the cool wind
Plays on the leaves: all be far away,
Since thou art far away; by whose dear side
How often have I sat Crown'd with fresh flowers
For summers Queen, whil'st every Shepherds Boy
Puts on his lusty green, with gaudy hook,
And hanging scrip of finest Cordevan.
But thou art gone, and these are gone with thee,
And all are dead but thy dear memorie;
That shall out-live thee, and shall ever spring
Whilest there are pipes, or jolly Shepherds sing.
And here will I in honour of thy love,
Dwell by thy Grave, forgeting all those joys,
That former times made precious to mine eyes,
Only remembring what my youth did gain
In the dark, hidden vertuous use of Herbs:
That will I practise, and as freely give
All my endeavours, as I gain'd them free.
Of all green wounds I know the remedies
In Men or Cattel, be they stung with Snakes,
Or charm'd with powerful words of wicked Art,
Or be they Love-sick, or through too much heat
Grown wild or Lunatick, their eyes or ears
Thickned with misty filme of dulling Rheum,

1

The Faithful Shepherdess

These I can Cure, such secret vertue lies
In Herbs applyed by a Virgins hand:
My meat shall be what these wild woods afford,
Berries, and Chesnuts, Plantanes, on whose Cheeks,
The Sun sits smiling, and the lofty fruit
Pull'd from the fair head of the staight grown Pine;
On these I'le feed with free content and rest,
When night shall blind the world, by thy side blest.

Enter a Satyr.

Satyr. Through yon same bending plain
That flings his arms down to the main,
And through these thick woods have I run,
Whose bottom never kist the Sun
Since the lusty Spring began,
All to please my master *Pan,*
Have I trotted without rest
To get him Fruit; for at a Feast
He entertains this coming night
His Paramour, the *Syrinx* bright:
But behold a fairer sight!   [*He stands amazed.*
By that Heavenly form of thine,
Brightest fair thou art divine,
Sprung from great immortal race
Of the gods, for in thy face
Shines more awful Majesty,
Than dull weak mortalitie
Dare with misty eyes behold,
And live: therefore on this mold
Lowly do I bend my knee,
In worship of thy Deitie;
Deign it Goddess from my hand,
To receive what e're this land
From her fertil Womb doth send
Of her choice Fruits: and but lend
Belief to that the Satyre tells,
Fairer by the famous wells,
To this present day ne're grew,
Never better nor more true.
Here be Grapes whose lusty bloud
Is the learned Poets good,
Sweeter yet did never crown

The head of *Bacchus*, Nuts more brown
Than the Squirrels Teeth that crack them;
Deign O fairest fair to take them.
For these black ey'd *Driope*
Hath oftentimes commanded me,
With my clasped knee to clime;
See how well the lusty time
Hath deckt their rising cheeks in red,
Such as on your lips is spred,
Here be Berries for a Queen,
Some be red, some be green,
These are of that luscious meat,
The great God *Pan* himself doth eat:
All these, and what the woods can yield,
The hanging mountain or the field,
I freely offer, and ere long
Will bring you more, more sweet and strong,
Till when humbly leave I take,
Lest the great *Pan* do awake,
That sleeping lies in a deep glade,
Under a broad Beeches shade,
I must go, I must run
Swifter than the fiery Sun.   [*Exit.*

Clo. And all my fears go with thee.
What greatness or what private hidden power,
Is there in me to draw submission
From this rude man, and beast? sure I am mortal:
The Daughter of a Shepherd, he was mortal:
And she that bore me mortal: prick my hand
And it will bleed: a Feaver shakes me,
And the self same wind that makes the young Lambs shrink,
Makes me a cold: my fear says I am mortal:
Yet I have heard (my Mother told it me)
And now I do believe it, if I keep
My Virgin Flower uncropt, pure, chaste, and fair,
No Goblin, Wood-god, Fairy, Elfe, or Fiend,
Satyr or other power that haunts the Groves,
Shall hurt my body, or by vain illusion
Draw me to wander after idle fires;
Or voyces calling me in dead of night,
To make me follow, and so tole me on
Through mire and standing pools, to find my ruine:

3

Else why should this rough thing, who never knew
Manners, nor smooth humanity, whose heats
Are rougher than himself, and more mishapen,
Thus mildly kneel to me? sure there is a power
In that great name of Virgin, that binds fast
All rude uncivil bloods, all appetites
That break their confines: then strong Chastity
Be thou my strongest guard, for here I'le dwell
In opposition against Fate and Hell.

Enter an old Shepherd, *with him four couple of* Shepherds
and Shepherdesses.

Old Shep. Now we have done this holy Festival
In honour of our great God, and his rites
Perform'd, prepare your selves for chaste
And uncorrupted fires: that as the Priest,
With powerful hand shall sprinkle on [your] Brows
His pure and holy water, ye may be
From all hot flames of lust, and loose thoughts free.
Kneel Shepherds, kneel, here comes the Priest of *Pan.*

Enter Priest.

Priest. Shepherds, thus I purge away,
Whatsoever this great day,
Or the past hours gave not good,
To corrupt your Maiden blood:
From the high rebellious heat
Of the Grapes, and strength of meat;
From the wanton quick desires,
They do kindle by their fires,
I do wash you with this water,
Be you pure and fair hereafter.
From your Liver and your Veins,
Thus I take away the stains.
All your thoughts be smooth and fair,
Be ye fresh and free as Air.
Never more let lustful heat
Through your purged conduits beat,
Or a plighted troth be broken,
Or a wanton verse be spoken
In a Shepherdesses ear;

The Faithful Shepherdess

Go your wayes, ye are all clear.
> [*They rise and sing in praise of* Pan.

The SONG.

Sing his praises that doth keep
  Our Flocks from harm,
Pan *the Father of our Sheep,*
  And arm in arm
Tread we softly in a round,
Whilest the hollow neighbouring ground
Fills the Musick with her sound.

Pan, O great God Pan, *to thee*
  Thus do we sing:
Thou that keep'st us chaste and free
  As the young spring,
Ever be thy honour spoke,
From that place the morn is broke,
To that place Day doth unyoke.
> [*Exeunt omnes but* Perigot *and* Amoret.

Peri. Stay gentle *Amoret,* thou fair brow'd Maid,
Thy Shepherd prays thee stay, that holds thee dear,
Equal with his souls good.

Amo. Speak; I give
Thee freedom Shepherd, and thy tongue be still
The same it ever was; as free from ill,
As he whose conversation never knew
The Court or City be thou ever true.

Peri. When I fall off from my affection,
Or mingle my clean thoughts with foul desires,
First let our great God cease to keep my flocks,
That being left alone without a guard,
The Wolf, or Winters rage, Summers great heat,
And want of Water, Rots; or what to us
Of ill is yet unknown, full speedily,
And in their general ruine let me feel.

Amo. I pray thee gentle Shepherd wish not so,
I do believe thee: 'tis as hard for me

To think thee false, and harder than for thee
To hold me foul.

Peri. O you are fairer far
Than the chaste blushing morn, or that fair star
That guides the wandring Sea-men through the deep,
Straighter than straightest Pine upon the steep
Head of an aged mountain, and more white
Than the new Milk we strip before day-light
From the full fraighted bags of our fair flocks:
Your hair more beauteous than those hanging locks
Of young *Apollo*.

Amo. Shepherd be not lost,
Y'are sail'd too far already from the Coast
Of our discourse.

Peri. Did you not tell me once
I should not love alone, I should not lose
Those many passions, vows, and holy Oaths,
I've sent to Heaven? did you not give your hand,
Even that fair hand in hostage? Do not then
Give back again those sweets to other men,
You your self vow'd were mine.

Amo. Shepherd, so far as Maidens modesty
May give assurance, I am once more thine,
Once more I give my hand; be ever free
From that great foe to faith, foul jealousie.

Peri. I take it as my best good, and desire
For stronger confirmation of our love,
To meet this happy night in that fair Grove,
Where all true Shepherds have rewarded been
For their long service: say sweet, shall it hold?

Amo. Dear friend, you must not blame me if I make
A doubt of what the silent night may do,
Coupled with this dayes heat to move your bloud:
Maids must be fearful; sure you have not been
Wash'd white enough; for yet I see a stain
Stick in your Liver, go and purge again.

The Faithful Shepherdess

Peri. O do not wrong my honest simple truth,
My self and my affections are as pure
As those chaste flames that burn before the shrine
Of the great *Dian*: only my intent
To draw you thither, was to plight our troths,
With enterchange of mutual chaste embraces,
And ceremonious tying of our selves:
For to that holy wood is consecrate
A vertuous well, about whose flowry banks,
The nimble-footed Fairies dance their rounds,
By the pale moon-shine, dipping oftentimes
Their stolen Children, so to make them free
From dying flesh, and dull mortalitie;
By this fair Fount hath many a Shepherd sworn,
And given away his freedom, many a troth
Been plight, which neither envy, nor old time
Could ever break, with many a chaste kiss given,
In hope of coming happiness; by this
Fresh Fountain many a blushing Maid
Hath crown'd the head of her long loved Shepherd
With gaudy flowers, whilest he happy sung
Layes of his love and dear Captivitie;
There grows all Herbs fit to cool looser flames
Our sensual parts provoke, chiding our bloods,
And quenching by their power those hidden sparks
That else would break out, and provoke our sense
To open fires, so vertuous is that place:
Then gentle Shepherdess, believe and grant,
In troth it fits not with that face to scant
Your faithful Shepherd of those chaste desires
He ever aim'd at, and —

Amo. Thou hast prevail'd, farewel, this coming night
Shall crown thy chast hopes with long wish'd delight.

Peri. Our great god *Pan* reward thee for that good
Thou hast given thy poor Shepherd: fairest Bud
Of Maiden Vertues, when I leave to be
The true Admirer of thy Chastitie,
Let me deserve the hot polluted Name
Of the wild Woodman, or affect: some Dame,
Whose often Prostitution hath begot
More foul Diseases, than ever yet the hot

7

The Faithful Shepherdess

Sun bred through his burnings, whilst the Dog
Pursues the raging Lion, throwing Fog,
And deadly Vapour from his angry Breath,
Filling the lower World with Plague and Death. [*Ex. Am.*

Hamlet

Enter Amaryllis.

Ama. Shepherd, may I desire to be believ'd,
What I shall blushing tell?

Peri. Fair Maid, you may.

Am. Then softly thus, I love thee, *Perigot*,
And would be gladder to be lov'd again,
Than the cold Earth is in his frozen arms
To clip the wanton Spring: nay do not start,
Nor wonder that I woo thee, thou that art
The prime of our young Grooms, even the top
Of all our lusty Shepherds! what dull eye
That never was acquainted with desire,
Hath seen thee wrastle, run, or cast the Stone
With nimble strength and fair delivery,
And hath not sparkled fire, and speedily
Sent secret heat to all the neighbouring Veins?
Who ever heard thee sing, that brought again
That freedom back, was lent unto thy Voice;
Then do not blame me (Shepherd) if I be
One to be numbred in this Companie,
Since none that ever saw thee yet, were free.

Peri. Fair Shepherdess, much pity I can lend
To your Complaints: but sure I shall not love:
All that is mine, my self, and my best hopes
Are given already; do not love him then
That cannot love again: on other men
Bestow those heats more free, that may return
You fire for fire, and in one flame equal burn.

Ama. Shall I rewarded be so slenderly
For my affection, most unkind of men!
If I were old, or had agreed with Art
To give another Nature to my Cheeks,
Or were I common Mistress to the love

Of every Swain, or could I with such ease
Call back my Love, as many a Wanton doth;
Thou might'st refuse me, Shepherd; but to thee
I am only fixt and set, let it not be
A Sport, thou gentle Shepherd to abuse
The love of silly Maid.

Peri. Fair Soul, ye use
These words to little end: for know, I may
Better call back that time was Yesterday,
Or stay the coming Night, than bring my Love
Home to my self again, or recreant prove.
I will no longer hold you with delays,
This present night I have appointed been
To meet that chaste Fair (that enjoys my Soul)
In yonder Grove, there to make up our Loves.
Be not deceiv'd no longer, chuse again,
These neighbouring Plains have many a comely Swain,
Fresher, and freer far than I e'r was,
Bestow that love on them, and let me pass.
Farewel, be happy in a better Choice.   [*Exit.*

Ama. Cruel, thou hast struck me deader with thy Voice
Than if the angry Heavens with their quick flames
Had shot me through: I must not leave to love,
I cannot, no I must enjoy thee, Boy,
Though the great dangers 'twixt my hopes and that
Be infinite: there is a Shepherd dwells
Down by the Moor, whose life hath ever shown
More sullen Discontent than *Saturns* Brow,
When he sits frowning on the Births of Men:
One that doth wear himself away in loneness;
And never joys unless it be in breaking
The holy plighted troths of mutual Souls:
One that lusts after [every] several Beauty,
But never yet was known to love or like,
Were the face fairer, or more full of truth,
Than *Phoebe* in her fulness, or the youth
Of smooth *Lyaeus*; whose nigh starved flocks
Are always scabby, and infect all Sheep
They feed withal; whose Lambs are ever last,
And dye before their waining, and whose Dog
Looks like his Master, lean, and full of scurf,

9

The Faithful Shepherdess

Not caring for the Pipe or Whistle: this man may
(If he be well wrought) do a deed of wonder,
Forcing me passage to my long desires:
And here he comes, as fitly to my purpose,
As my quick thoughts could wish for.

Enter Shepherd.

Shep. Fresh Beauty, let me not be thought uncivil,
Thus to be Partner of your loneness: 'twas
My Love (that ever working passion) drew
Me to this place to seek some remedy
For my sick Soul: be not unkind and fair,
For such the mighty Cupid in his doom
Hath sworn to be aveng'd on; then give room
To my consuming Fires, that so I may
Enjoy my long Desires, and so allay
Those flames that else would burn my life away.

Ama. Shepherd, were I but sure thy heart were sound
As thy words seem to be, means might be found
To cure thee of thy long pains; for to me
That heavy youth-consuming Miserie
The love-sick Soul endures, never was pleasing;
I could be well content with the quick easing
Of thee, and thy hot fires, might it procure
Thy faith and farther service to be sure.

Shep. Name but that great work, danger, or what can
Be compass'd by the Wit or Art of Man,
And if I fail in my performance, may
I never more kneel to the rising Day.

Ama. Then thus I try thee, Shepherd, this same night,
That now comes stealing on, a gentle pair
Have promis'd equal Love, and do appoint
To make yon Wood the place where hands and hearts
Are to be ty'd for ever: break their meeting
And their strong Faith, and I am ever thine.

Shep. Tell me their Names, and if I do not move
(By my great power) the Centre of their Love
From his fixt being, let me never more

Warm me by those fair Eyes I thus adore.

Ama. Come, as we go, I'll tell thee what they are,
And give thee fit directions for thy work.   [*Exeunt.*

Enter Cloe.

Cloe. How have I wrong'd the times, or men, that thus
After this holy Feast I pass unknown
And unsaluted? 'twas not wont to be
Thus frozen with the younger companie
Of jolly Shepherds; 'twas not then held good,
For lusty Grooms to mix their quicker blood
With that dull humour, most unfit to be
The friend of man, cold and dull Chastitie.
Sure I am held not fair, or am too old,
Or else not free enough, or from my fold
Drive not a flock sufficient great, to gain
The greedy eyes of wealth-alluring Swain:
Yet if I may believe what others say,
My face has soil enough; nor can they lay
Justly too strict a Coyness to my Charge;
My Flocks are many, and the Downs as large
They feed upon: then let it ever be
Their Coldness, not my Virgin Modestie
Makes me complain.

Enter Thenot.

The. Was ever Man but I
Thus truly taken with uncertainty?
Where shall that Man be found that loves a mind
Made up in Constancy, and dare not find
His Love rewarded? here let all men know
A Wretch that lives to love his Mistress so.

Clo. Shepherd, I pray thee stay, where hast thou been?
Or whither go'st thou? here be Woods as green
As any, air likewise as fresh and sweet,
As where smooth *Zephyrus* plays on the fleet
Face of the curled Streams, with Flowers as many
As the young Spring gives, and as choise as any;
Here be all new Delights, cool Streams and Wells,

The Faithful Shepherdess

Arbors o'rgrown with Woodbinds, Caves, and Dells,
Chase where thou wilt, whilst I sit by, and sing,
Or gather Rushes to make many a Ring
For thy long fingers; tell thee tales of Love,
How the pale *Phoebe* hunting in a Grove,
First saw the Boy *Endymion*, from whose Eyes
She took eternal fire that never dyes;
How she convey'd him softly in a sleep,
His temples bound with poppy to the steep
Head of old *Latmus*, where she stoops each night,
Gilding the Mountain with her Brothers light,
To kiss her sweetest.

The. Far from me are these
Hot flashes, bred from wanton heat and ease;
I have forgot what love and loving meant:
Rhimes, Songs, and merry Rounds, that oft are sent
To the soft Ears of Maids, are strange to me;
Only I live t' admire a Chastitie,
That neither pleasing Age, smooth tongue, or Gold,
Could ever break upon, so pure a Mold
Is that her Mind was cast in; 'tis to her
I only am reserv'd; she is my form I stir
By, breath and move, 'tis she and only she
Can make me happy, or give miserie.

Clo. Good Shepherd, may a Stranger crave to know
To whom this dear observance you do ow?

The. You may, and by her Vertue learn to square
And level out your Life; for to be fair
And nothing vertuous, only fits the Eye
Of gaudy Youth, and swelling Vanitie.
Then know, she's call'd the Virgin of the Grove,
She that hath long since bury'd her chaste Love,
And now lives by his Grave, for whose dear Soul
She hath vow'd her self into the holy Roll
Of strict Virginity; 'tis her I so admire,
Not any looser Blood, or new desire.

Clo. Farewel poor Swain, thou art not for my bend,
I must have quicker Souls, whose works may tend
To some free action: give me him dare love

At first encounter, and as soon dare prove.

The SONG.

  Come Shepherds, come,
Come away without delay
Whilst the gentle time dot[h] stay.
  Green Woods are dumb,
And will never tell to any
Those dear Kisses, and those many
Sweet Embraces that are given
Dainty Pleasures that would even
Raise in coldest Age a fire,
And give Virgin Blood desire,
    Then if ever,
    Now or never,
    Come and have it,
    Think not I,
    Dare deny,
    If you crave it.

Enter Daphnis.

Here comes another: better be my speed,
Thou god of Blood: but certain, if I read
Not false, this is that modest Shepherd, he
That only dare salute, but ne'r could be
Brought to kiss any, hold discourse, or sing,
Whisper, or boldly ask that wished thing
We all are born for; one that makes loving Faces,
And could be well content to covet Graces,
Were they not got by boldness; in this thing
My hopes are frozen; and but Fate doth bring
Him hither, I would sooner chuse
A Man made out of Snow, and freer use
An Eunuch to my ends: but since he's here,
Thus I attempt him. Thou of men most dear,
Welcome to her, that only for thy sake,
Hath been content to live: here boldly take
My hand in pledg, this hand, that never yet
Was given away to any: and but sit
Down on this rushy Bank, whilst I go pull
Fresh Blossoms from the Boughs, or quickly cull

The Faithful Shepherdess

The choicest delicates from yonder Mead,
To make thee Chains, or Chaplets, or to spread
Under our fainting Bodies, when delight
Shall lock up all our senses. How the sight
Of those smooth rising Cheeks renew the story
Of young *Adonis*, when in Pride and Glory
He lay infolded 'twixt the beating arms
Of willing *Venus*: methinks stronger Charms
Dwell in those speaking eyes, and on that brow
More sweetness than the Painters can allow
To their best pieces: not *Narcissus*, he
That wept himself away in memorie
Of his own Beauty, nor *Silvanus* Boy,
Nor the twice ravish'd Maid, for whom old *Troy*
Fell by the hand of *Pirrhus*, may to thee
Be otherwise compar'd, than some dead Tree
To a young fruitful Olive.

Daph. I can love,
But I am loth to say so, lest I prove
Too soon unhappy.

Clo. Happy thou would'st say,
My dearest *Daphnis*, blush not, if the day
To thee and thy soft heats be enemie,
Then take the coming Night, fair youth 'tis free
To all the World, Shepherd, I'll meet thee then
When darkness hath shut up the eyes of men,
In yonder Grove: speak, shall our Meeting hold?
Indeed you are too bashful, be more bold,
And tell me I.

Daph. I'm content to say so,
And would be glad to meet, might I but pray so
Much from your Fairness, that you would be true.

Clo. Shepherd, thou hast thy Wish.

Daph. Fresh Maid, adieu:
Yet one word more, since you have drawn me on
To come this Night, fear not to meet alone
That man that will not offer to be ill,
Though your bright self would ask it, for his fill

The Faithful Shepherdess

Of this Worlds goodness: do not fear him then,
But keep your 'pointed time; let other men
Set up their Bloods to sale, mine shall be ever
Fair as the Soul it carries, and unchast never.   [*Exit.*

Clo. Yet am I poorer than I was before.
Is it not strange, among so many a score
Of lusty Bloods, I should pick out these things
Whose Veins like a dull River far from Springs,
Is still the same, slow, heavy, and unfit
For stream or motion, though the strong winds hit
With their continual power upon his sides?
O happy be your names that have been brides,
And tasted those rare sweets for which I pine:
And far more heavy be thy grief and time,
Thou lazie swain, that maist relieve my needs,
Than his, upon whose liver alwayes feeds
A hungry vultur.

Enter Alexis.

Ale. Can such beauty be
Safe in his own guard, and not draw the eye
Of him that passeth on, to greedy gaze,
Or covetous desire, whilst in a maze
The better part contemplates, giving rein
And wished freedom to the labouring vein?
Fairest and whitest, may I crave to know
The cause of your retirement, why ye goe
Thus all alone? methinks the downs are sweeter,
And the young company of swains far meeter,
Than those forsaken and untroden places.
Give not your self to loneness, and those graces
Hid from the eyes of men, that were intended
To live amongst us swains.

Cloe. Thou art befriended,
Shepherd, in all my life I have not seen
A man in whom greater contents have been
Than thou thy self art: I could tell thee more,
Were there but any hope left to restore
My freedom lost. O lend me all thy red,
Thou shamefast morning, when from *Tithons* bed

15

Thou risest ever maiden.

Alex. If for me,
Thou sweetest of all sweets, these flashes be,
Speak and be satisfied. O guide her tongue,
My better angel; force my name among
Her modest thoughts, that the first word may be—

Cloe. Alexis, when the sun shall kiss the Sea,
Taking his rest by the white *Thetis* side,
Meet in the holy wood, where I'le abide
Thy coming, Shepherd.

Alex. If I stay behind,
An everlasting dulness, and the wind,
That as he passeth by shuts up the stream
Of *Rhine* or *Volga*, whilst the suns hot beam
Beats back again, seise me, and let me turn
To coldness more than ice: oh how I burn
And rise in youth and fire! I dare not stay.

Cloe. My name shall be your word.

Alex. Fly, fly thou day.   [*Exit.*

Cloe. My grief is great if both these boyes should fail:
He that will use all winds must shift his sail.   [*Exit.*

16

The Faithful Shepherdess

Actus Secundus. Scena Prima.

Enter an old Shepherd, *with a bell ringing, and the Priest of Pan following.*

Priest. O Shepherds all, and maidens fair,
Fold your flocks up, for the Air
'Gins to thicken, and the sun
Already his great course hath run.
See the dew-drops how they kiss
Every little flower that is:
Hanging on their velvet heads,
Like a rope of crystal beads.
See the heavy clouds low falling,
And bright *Hesperus* down calling
The dead night from under ground,
At whose rising mists unsound, → Humbld
Damps, and vapours fly apace,
Hovering o're the wanton face
Of these pastures, where they come,
Striking dead both bud and bloom;
Therefore from such danger lock
Every one his loved flock,
And let your Dogs lye loose without,
Lest the Wolf come as a scout
From the mountain, and e're day
Bear a Lamb or kid away,
Or the crafty theevish Fox,
Break upon your simple flocks:
To secure your selves from these,
Be not too secure in ease;
Let one eye his watches keep,
Whilst the t'other eye doth sleep;
So you shall good Shepherds prove,
And for ever hold the love
Of our great god. Sweetest slumbers
And soft silence fall in numbers
On your eye-lids: so farewel,
Thus I end my evenings knel.   [*Exeunt.*

Enter Clorin, *the* Shepherdess, *sorting of herbs, and telling the natures of them.*

Clor. Now let me know what my best Art hath done,
Helpt by the great power of the vertuous moon
In her full light; O you sons of Earth,
You only brood, unto whose happy birth
Vertue was given, holding more of nature
Than man her first born and most perfect creature,
Let me adore you; you that only can
Help or kill nature, drawing out that span
Of life and breath even to the end of time;
You that these hands did crop, long before prime
Of day; give me your names, and next your hidden power.
This is the *Clote* bearing a yellow flower,
And this black Horehound, both are very good
For sheep or Shepherd, bitten by a wood-
Dogs venom'd tooth; these Ramuns branches are,
Which stuck in entries, or about the bar
That holds the door fast, kill all inchantments, charms,
Were they *Medeas* verses that doe harms
To men or cattel; these for frenzy be
A speedy and a soveraign remedie,
The bitter Wormwood, Sage, and Marigold,
Such sympathy with mans good they do hold;
This Tormentil, whose vertue is to part
All deadly killing poyson from the heart;
And here *Narcissus* roots for swellings be:
Yellow *Lysimacus*, to give sweet rest
To the faint Shepherd, killing where it comes
All busie gnats, and every fly that hums:
For leprosie, Darnel, and Sellondine,
With Calamint, whose vertues do refine
The blood of man, making it free and fair
As the first hour it breath'd, or the best air.
Here other two, but your rebellious use
Is not for me, whose goodness is abuse;
Therefore foul Standergrass, from me and mine
I banish thee, with lustful Turpentine,
You that intice the veins and stir the heat
To civil mutiny, scaling the seat
Our reason moves in, and deluding it
With dreams and wanton fancies, till the fit
Of burning lust be quencht; by appetite,
Robbing the soul of blessedness and light:
And thou light *Varvin* too, thou must go after,

Provoking easie souls to mirth and laughter;
No more shall I dip thee in water now,
And sprinkle every post, and every bough
With thy well pleasing juyce, to make the grooms
Swell with high mirth, as with joy all the rooms.

Enter Thenot.

The. This is the Cabin where the best of all
Her Sex, that ever breath'd, or ever shall
Give heat or happiness to the Shepherds side,
Doth only to her worthy self abide.
Thou blessed star, I thank thee for thy light,
Thou by whose power the darkness of sad night
Is banisht from the Earth, in whose dull place
Thy chaster beams play on the heavy face
Of all the world, making the blue Sea smile,
To see how cunningly thou dost beguile
Thy Brother of his brightness, giving day
Again from *Chaos*, whiter than that way
That leads to *Joves* high Court, and chaster far
Than chastity it self, yon blessed star
That nightly shines: Thou, all the constancie
That in all women was, or e're shall be,
From whose fair eye-balls flyes that holy fire,
That Poets stile the Mother of desire,
Infusing into every gentle brest
A soul of greater price, and far more blest
Than that quick power, which gives a difference,
'Twixt man and creatures of a lower sense.

Clor. Shepherd, how cam'st thou hither to this place?
No way is troden, all the verdant grass
The spring shot up, stands yet unbruised here
Of any foot, only the dapled Deer
Far from the feared sound of crooked horn
Dwels in this fastness.

Th. Chaster than the morn,
I have not wandred, or by strong illusion
Into this vertuous place have made intrusion:
But hither am I come (believe me fair)
To seek you out, of whose great good the air

19

The Faithful Shepherdess

Is full, and strongly labours, whilst the sound
Breaks against Heaven, and drives into a stound
The amazed Shepherd, that such vertue can
Be resident in lesser than a man.

Clor. If any art I have, or hidden skill
May cure thee of disease or festred ill,
Whose grief or greenness to anothers eye
May seem impossible of remedy,
I dare yet undertake it.

The. 'Tis no pain
I suffer through disease, no beating vein
Conveyes infection dangerous to the heart,
No part impostum'd to be cur'd by Art,
This body holds; and yet a feller grief
Than ever skilfull hand did give relief
Dwells on my soul, and may be heal'd by you,
Fair beauteous Virgin.

Clor. Then Shepherd, let me sue
To know thy grief; that man yet never knew
The way to health, that durst not shew his sore.

Then. Then fairest, know, I love you.

C[l]or. Swain, no more,
Thou hast abus'd the strictness of this place,
And offred Sacrilegious foul disgrace
To the sweet rest of these interred bones,
For fear of whose ascending, fly at once,
Thou and thy idle passions, that the sight
Of death and speedy vengeance may not fright
Thy very soul with horror.

Then. Let me not
(Thou all perfection) merit such a blot
For my true zealous faith.

Clor. Dar'st thou abide
To see this holy Earth at once divide
And give her body up? for sure it will,
If thou pursu'st with wanton flames to fill

The Faithful Shepherdess

This hallowed place; therefore repent and goe,
Whilst I with praise appease his Ghost below,
That else would tell thee what it were to be
A rival in that vertuous love that he
Imbraces yet.

Then. 'Tis not the white or red
Inhabits in your cheek that thus can wed
My mind to adoration; nor your eye,
Though it be full and fair, your forehead high,
And smooth as *Pelops* shoulder; not the smile
Lies watching in those dimples to beguile
The easie soul, your hands and fingers long
With veins inamel'd richly, nor your tongue,
Though it spoke sweeter than *Arions* Harp,
Your hair wove into many a curious warp,
Able in endless errour to infold
The wandring soul, nor the true perfect mould
Of all your body, which as pure doth show
In Maiden whiteness as the Alpsian snow.
All these, were but your constancie away,
Would please me less than a black stormy day
The wretched Seaman toyling through the deep.
But whilst this honour'd strictness you dare keep,
Though all the plagues that e're begotten were
In the great womb of air, were setled here,
In opposition, I would, like the tree,
Shake off those drops of weakness, and be free
Even in the arm of danger.

Clor. Wouldst thou have
Me raise again (fond man) from silent grave,
Those sparks that long agoe were buried here,
With my dead friends cold ashes?

Then. Dearest dear,
I dare not ask it, nor you must not grant;
Stand strongly to your vow, and do not faint:
Remember how he lov'd ye, and be still
The same Opinion speaks ye; let not will,
And that great god of women, appetite,
Set up your blood again; do not invite
Desire and fancie from their long exile,

To set them once more in a pleasing smile:
Be like a rock made firmly up 'gainst all
The power of angry Heaven, or the strong fall
Of *Neptunes* battery; if ye yield, I die
To all affection; 'tis that loyaltie
Ye tie unto this grave I so admire;
And yet there's something else I would desire,
If you would hear me, but withall deny.
O *Pan*, what an uncertain destiny
Hangs over all my hopes! I will retire,
For if I longer stay, this double fire
Will lick my life up.

Clor. Doe, let time wear out
What Art and Nature cannot bring about.

Then. Farewel thou soul of vertue, and be blest
For ever, whilst that here I wretched rest
Thus to my self; yet grant me leave to dwell
In kenning of this Arbor; yon same dell
O'retopt with morning Cypress and sad Yew
Shall be my Cabin, where I'le early rew,
Before the Sun hath kist this dew away,
The hard uncertain chance which Fate doth lay
Upon this head.

Clor. The gods give quick release
And happy cure unto thy hard disease.   [*Exeunt*.

Enter Sullen Shepherd.

Sullen. I do not love this wench that I should meet,
For ne'r did my unconstant eye yet greet
That beauty, were it sweeter or more fair,
Than the new blossoms, when the morning air
Blows gently on the[m], or the breaking light,
When many maiden blushes to our sight
Shoot from his early face: were all these set
In some neat form before me, 'twould not get
The least love from me; some desire it might,
Or present burning: all to me in sight
Are equal, be they fair, or black, or brown,
Virgin, or careless wanton, I can crown

22

My appetite with any; swear as oft
And weep, as any, melt my words as soft
Into a maiden[s] ears, and tell how long
My heart has been her servant, and how strong
My passions are: call her unkind and cruel,
Offer her all I have to gain the Jewel
Maidens so highly prize: then loath, and fly:
This do I hold a blessed destiny.

Enter Amaryllis.

Amar. Hail Shepherd, *Pan* bless both thy flock and thee,
For being mindful of thy word to me.

Sul. Welcom fair Shepherdess, thy loving swain
Gives thee the self same wishes back again,
Who till this present hour ne're knew that eye,
Could make me cross mine arms, or daily dye
With fresh consumings: boldly tell me then,
How shall we part their faithful loves, and when?
Shall I bely him to her, shall I swear
His faith is false, and he loves every where?
I'le say he mockt her th' other day to you,
Which will by your confirming shew as true,
For he is of so pure an honesty,
To think (because he will not) none will lye:
Or else to him I'le slander *Amoret*,
And say, she but seems chaste; I'le swear she met
Me 'mongst the shady Sycamores last night
And loosely offred up her flame and spright
Into my bosom, made a wanton bed
Of leaves and many flowers, where she spread
Her willing body to be prest by me;
There have I carv'd her name on many a tree,
Together with mine own; to make this show
More full of seeming, *Hobinall* you know,
Son to the aged Shepherd of the glen,
Him I have sorted out of many men,
To say he found us at our private sport,
And rouz'd us 'fore our time by his resort:
This to confirm, I have promis'd to the boy
Many a pretty knack, and many a toy,
As gins to catch him birds, with bow and bolt,

23

The Faithful Shepherdess

To shoot at nimble Squirrels in the holt;
A pair of painted Buskins, and a Lamb,
Soft as his own locks, or the down of swan;
This I have done to win ye, which doth give
Me double pleasure. Discord makes me live.

Amar. Lov'd swain, I thank ye, these tricks might prevail
With other rustick Shepherds, but will fail
Even once to stir, much more to overthrow
His fixed love from judgement, who doth know
Your nature, my end, and his chosens merit;
Therefore some stranger way must force his spirit,
Which I have found: give second, and my love
Is everlasting thine.

Sul. Try me and prove.

Amar. These happy pair of lovers meet straightway,
Soon as they fold their flocks up with the day,
In the thick grove bordering upon yon Hill,
In whose hard side Nature hath carv'd a well,
And but that matchless spring which Poets know,
Was ne're the like to this: by it doth grow
About the sides, all herbs which Witches use,
All simples good for Medicine or abuse,
All sweets that crown the happy Nuptial day,
With all their colours, there the month of *May*
Is ever dwelling, all is young and green,
There's not a grass on which was ever seen
The falling *Autumn*, or cold Winters hand,
So full of heat and vertue is the land,
About this fountain, which doth slowly break
Below yon Mountains foot, into a Creek
That waters all the vally, giving Fish
Of many sorts, to fill the Shepherds dish.
This holy well, my grandam that is dead,
Right wise in charms, hath often to me said,
Hath power to change the form of any creature,
Being thrice dipt o're the head, into what feature,
Or shape 'twould please the letter down to crave,
Who must pronounce this charm too, which she gave
Me on her death-bed; told me what, and how,
I should apply unto the Patients brow,

That would be chang'd, casting them thrice asleep,
Before I trusted them into this deep.
All this she shew'd me, and did charge me prove
This secret of her Art, if crost in love.
I'le this attempt; now Shepherd, I have here
All her prescriptions, and I will not fear
To be my self dipt: come, my temples bind
With these sad herbs, and when I sleep you find,
As you do speak your charm, thrice down me let,
And bid the water raise me *Amoret*;
Which being done, leave me to my affair,
And e're the day shall quite it self out-wear,
I will return unto my Shepherds arm,
Dip me again, and then repeat this charm,
And pluck me up my self, whom freely take,
And the hotst fire of thine affection slake.

Sul. And if I fit thee not, then fit not me:
I long the truth of this wells power to see.   [*Exeunt.*

Enter Daphnis.

Daph. Here will I stay, for this the covert is
Where I appointed *Cloe*; do not miss,
Thou bright-ey'd virgin, come, O come my fair,
Be not abus'd with fear, nor let cold care
Of honour stay thee from the Shepherds arm,
Who would as hard be won to offer harm
To thy chast thoughts, as whiteness from the day,
Or yon great round to move another way.
My language shall be honest, full of truth,
My flames as smooth and spotless as my youth:
I will not entertain that wandring thought,
Whose easie current may at length be brought
To a loose vastness.

Alexis within. Cloe!

Daph. 'Tis her voyce,
And I must answer, *Cloe*! Oh the choice
Of dear embraces, chast and holy strains
Our hands shall give! I charge you all my veins
Through which the blood and spirit take their way,

25

Lock up your disobedient heats, and stay
Those mutinous desires that else would grow
To strong rebellion: do not wilder show
Than blushing modesty may entertain.

Alexis within. Cloe!

Daph. There sounds that [blessed] name again,

Enter Alexis.

And I will meet it: let me not mistake,
This is some Shepherd! sure I am awake;
What may this riddle mean? I will retire,
To give my self more knowledg.

Alex. Oh my fire,
How thou consum'st me! *Cloe,* answer me,
Alexis, strong *Alexis* , high and free,
Calls upon *Cloe.* See mine arms are full
Of entertainment, ready for to pull
That golden fruit which too too long hath hung
Tempting the greedy eye: thou stayest too long,
I am impatient of these mad delayes;
I must not leave unsought these many ways
That lead into this center, till I find
Quench for my burning lust. I come, unkind.   [*Exit* Alexis.

Daph. Can my imagination work me so much ill,
That I may credit this for truth, and still
Believe mine eyes? or shall I firmly hold
Her yet untainted, and these sights but bold
Illusion? Sure such fancies oft have been
Sent to abuse true love, and yet are seen,
Daring to blind the vertuous thought with errour.
But be they far from me with their fond terrour:
I am resolv'd my *Cloe* yet is true.   [Cloe *within.*
Cloe, hark, *Cloe:* Sure this voyce is new,
Whose shrilness like the sounding of a Bell,
Tells me it is a Woman: *Cloe,* tell
Thy blessed name again. *Cloe.* [*within*] Here.
Oh what a grief is this to be so near,
And not incounter!

Enter Cloe.

Clo. Shepherd, we are met,
Draw close into the covert, lest the wet
Which falls like lazy mists upon the ground
Soke through your Startups.

Daph. Fairest are you found?
How have we wandred, that the better part
Of this good night is perisht? Oh my heart!
How have I long'd to meet ye, how to kiss
Those lilly hands, how to receive the bliss
That charming tongue gives to the happy ear
Of him that drinks your language! but I fear
I am too much unmanner'd, far too rude,
And almost grown lascivious to intrude
These hot behaviours; where regard of fame,
Honour, and modesty, a vertuous name,
And such discourse as one fair Sister may
Without offence unto the Brother say,
Should rather have been tendred: but believe,
Here dwells a better temper; do not grieve
Then, ever kindest, that my first salute
Seasons so much of fancy, I am mute
Henceforth to all discourses, but shall be
Suiting to your sweet thoughts and modestie.
Indeed I will not ask a kiss of you,
No not to wring your fingers, nor to sue
To those blest pair of fixed stars for smiles,
All a young lovers cunning, all his wiles,
And pretty wanton dyings, shall to me
Be strangers; only to your chastitie
I am devoted ever.

Clo. Honest Swain,
First let me thank you, then return again
As much of my love: no thou art too cold,
Unhappy Boy, not tempred to my mold,
Thy blood falls heavy downward, 'tis not fear
To offend in boldness wins, they never wear
Deserved favours that deny to take
When they are offered freely: Do I wake
To see a man of his youth, years and feature,

27

And such a one as we call goodly creature,
Thus backward? What a world of precious Art
Were meerly lost, to make him do his part?
But I will shake him off, that dares not hold,
Let men that hope to be belov'd be bold.
Daphnis, I do desire, since we are met
So happily, our lives and fortunes set
Upon one stake, to give assurance now,
By interchange of hands and holy vow,
Never to break again: walk you that way
Whilest I in zealous meditation stray
A little this way: when we both have ended
These rites and duties, by the woods befriended,
And secrecie of night, retire and find
An aged Oak, whose hollowness may bind
Us both within his body, thither go,
It stands within yon bottom.

Daph. Be it so.   [*Ex.* Daph.

Clo. And I will meet there never more with thee,
Thou idle shamefastness.

Alex. [*within*] Chloe!

Clo. 'Tis he
That dare I hope be bolder.

Alex. Cloe!

Clo. Now
Great *Pan* for *Syrinx* sake bid speed our Plow.   [*Exit* Cloe.

The Faithful Shepherdess

Actus Tertius. Scena Prima.

Enter Sullen Shepherd *with* Amaryllis *in a sleep.*

Sull. From thy forehead thus I take
These herbs, and charge thee not awake
Till in yonder holy Well,
Thrice with powerful Magick spell,
Fill'd with many a baleful word,
Thou hast been dipt; thus with my cord
Of blasted Hemp, by Moon-light twin'd,
I do thy sleepy body bind;
I turn thy head into the East,
And thy feet into the West,
Thy left arm to the South put forth,
And thy right unto the North:
I take thy body from the ground,
In this deep and deadly swound,
And into this holy spring
I let thee slide down by my string.
Take this Maid thou holy pit,
To thy bottom, nearer yet,
In thy water pure and sweet,
By thy leave I dip her feet;
Thus I let her lower yet,
That her ankles may be wet;
Yet down lower, let her knee
In thy waters washed be;
There stop: Fly away
Every thing that loves the day.
Truth that hath but one face,
Thus I charm thee from this place.
Snakes that cast your coats for new,
Camelions that alter hue,
Hares that yearly Sexes change,
Proteus alt'ring oft and strange,
Hecate with shapes three,
Let this Maiden changed be,
With this holy water wet,
To the shape of *Amoret*:
Cynthia work thou with my charm,
Thus I draw thee free from harm

Up out of this blessed Lake,
Rise both like her and awake.   [*She awakes.*

Amar. Speak Shepherd, am I *Amoret* to sight?
Or hast thou mist in any Magick rite;
For want of which any defect in me,
May make our practices discovered be.

Sul. By yonder Moon, but that I here do stand,
Whose breath hath thus transform'd thee, and whose hand
Let thee down dry, and pluckt thee up thus wet,
I should my self take thee for *Amoret*;
Thou art in cloths, in feature, voice and hew
So like, that sense cannot distinguish you.

Amar. Then this deceit which cannot crossed be,
At once shall lose her him, and gain thee me.
Hither she needs must come by promise made,
And sure his nature never was so bad,
To bid a Virgin meet him in the wood,
When night and fear are up, but understood,
'Twas his part to come first: being come, I'le say,
My constant love made me come first and stay,
Then will I lead him further to the grove,
But stay you here, and if his own true love
Shall seek him here, set her in some wrong path,
Which say, her lover lately troden hath;
I'le not be far from hence, if need there be,
Here is another charm, whose power will free
The dazeled sense, read by the Moons beams clear,
And in my own true map make me appear.

Enter Perigot.

Sull. Stand close, here's *Perigot*, whose constant heart
Longs to behold her in whose shape thou art.

Per. This is the place (fair *Amoret*) the hour
Is yet scarce come: Here every Sylvan power
Delights to be about yon sacred Well,
Which they have blest with many a powerful Spell;
For never Traveller in dead of Night,
Nor strayed Beasts have faln in, but when sight

30

Hath fail'd them, then their right way they have found
By help of them, so holy is the ground:
But I will farther seek, lest *Amoret*
Should be first come, and so stray long unmet.
My *Amoret, Amoret.*   [*Ex.* Amaryllis, Perigot.

Per. My Love.

Amar. I come my Love.   [*Exit.*

Sull. Now she has got
Her own desires, and I shall gainer be
Of my long lookt for hopes as well as she.
How bright the moon shines here, as if she strove
To show her Glory in this little Grove,

Enter Amoret.

To some new loved Shepherd. Yonder is
Another *Amoret.* Where differs this
From that? but that she *Perigot* hath met,
I should have ta'n this for the counterfeit:
Herbs, Woods, and Springs, the power that in you lies,
If mortal men could know your Properties!

Amo. Methinks it is not Night, I have no fear,
Walking this Wood, of Lions, or the Bear,
Whose Names at other times have made me quake,
When any Shepherdess in her tale spake
Of some of them, that underneath a Wood
Have torn true Lovers that together stood.
Methinks there are no Goblins, and mens talk,
That in these Woods the nimble Fairies walk,
Are fables; such a strong heart I have got,
Because I come to meet with *Perigot.*
My *Perigot!* who's that, my *Perigot?*

Sull. Fair maid.

Amo. Ay me, thou art not *Perigot.*

Sull. But I can tell ye news of *Perigot*:
An hour together under yonder tree

He sate with wreathed arms and call'd on thee,
And said, why *Amoret* stayest thou so long?
Then starting up, down yonder path he flung,
Lest thou hadst miss'd thy way: were it day light,
He could not yet have born him out of sight.

Amor. Thanks, gentle Shepherd, and beshrew my stay,
That made me fearful I had lost my way:
As fast as my weak Legs (that cannot be
Weary with seeking him) will carry me,
I'll seek him out; and for thy Courtesie
Pray *Pan* thy Love may ever follow thee.   [*Exit.*

Sull. How bright she was, how lovely did she show!
Was it not pity to deceive her so?
She pluckt her Garments up, and tript away,
And with her Virgin-innocence did pray
For me that perjur'd her. Whilst she was here,
Methought the Beams of Light that did appear
Were shot from her; methought the Moon gave none,
But what it had from her: she was alone
With me, if then her presence did so move,
Why did not I essay to win her Love?
She would not sure have yielded unto me;
Women love only Opportunitie,
And not the Man; or if she had deny'd,
Alone, I might have forc'd her to have try'd
Who had been stronger: O vain Fool, to let
Such blest Occasion pass; I'll follow yet,
My Blood is up, I cannot now forbear.

Enter Alex, *and* Cloe.

I come sweet *Amoret*: Soft who is here?
A pair of Lovers? He shall yield her me;
"Now Lust is up, alike all Women be.

Alex. Where shall we rest? but for the love of me,
Cloe, I know ere this would weary be.

Clo. Alexis, let us rest here, if the place
Be private, and out of the common trace
Of every Shepherd: for I understood

The Faithful Shepherdess

This Night a number are about the Wood:
Then let us chuse some place, where out of sight
We freely may enjoy our stoln delight.

Alex. Then boldly here, where we shall ne're be found,
No Shepherds way lies here, 'tis hallow'd ground:
No Maid seeks here her strayed Cow, or Sheep,
Fairies, and Fawns, and Satyrs do it keep:
Then carelesly rest here, and clip and kiss,
And let no fear make us our pleasures miss.

Clo. Then lye by me, the sooner we begin,
The longer ere the day descry our sin.

Sull. Forbear to touch my Love, or by yon flame,
The greatest power that Shepherds dare to name,
Here where thou sit'st under this holy tree
Her to dishonour, thou shalt buried be.

Alex. If *Pan* himself, should come out of the lawns,
With all his Troops of Satyrs and of Fawns,
And bid me leave, I swear by her two eyes,
A greater Oath than thine, I would not rise.

Sull. Then from the cold Earth never shalt thou move,
But lose at one stroke both thy Life and Love.

Clo. Hold gentle Shepherd.

Sull. Fairest Shepherdess,
Come you with me, I do not love you less
Than that fond man, that would have kept you there
From me of more desert.

Alex. O yet forbear
To take her from me; give me leave to dye
By her.

[*The Satyr enters, he runs one way, and she another*.

Sat. Now whilst the Moon doth rule the Skie,
And the Stars, whose feeble light
Give a pale Shadow to the night,

Are up, great *Pan* commanded me
To walk this Grove about, whilst he
In a corner of the Wood,
Where never mortal foot hath stood,
Keeps dancing, musick, and a feast
To entertain a lovely Guest,
Where he gives her many a Rose,
Sweeter than the breath that blows
The leaves; Grapes, Berries of the best,
I never saw so great a feast.
But to my Charge: here must I stay,
To see what mortals lose their way,
And by a false fire seeming bright,
Train them in and leave them right.
Then must I watch if any be
Forcing of a Chastitie:
If I find it, then in haste
Give my wreathed horn a Blast,
And the Fairies all will run,
Wildly dancing by the Moon,
And will pinch him to the bone,
Till his lustful thoughts be gone.

Alex. O Death!

Sat. Back again about this ground,
Sure I hear a mortal sound;
I bind thee by this powerful Spell,
By the Waters of this Well,
By the glimmering Moon beams bright,
Speak again, thou mortal wight.

Alex. Oh!

Sat. Here the foolish mortal lies,
Sleeping on the ground: arise.
The poor wight is almost dead,
On the ground his wounds have bled,
And his cloaths foul'd with his blood:
To my Goddess in the Wood
Will I lead him, whose hands pure,
Will help this mortal wight to cure.

Enter Cloe *again.*

Clo. Since I beheld yon shaggy man, my Breast
Doth pant, each bush, methinks, should hide a Beast:
Yet my desire keeps still above my fear,
I would fain meet some Shepherd, knew I where:
For from one cause of fear I am most free,
It is impossible to ravish me,
I am so willing. Here upon this ground
I left my Love all bloody with his wound;
Yet till that fearful shape made me be gone,
Though he were hurt, I furnisht was of one,
But now both lost. *Alexis*, speak or move,
If thou hast any life, thou art yet my Love.
He's dead, or else is with his little might
Crept from the Bank for fear of that ill Spright.
Then where art thou that struck'st my love? O stay,
Bring me thy self in change, and then I'll say
Thou hast some justice, I will make thee trim
With Flowers and Garlands that were meant for him;
I'll clip thee round with both mine arms, as fast
As I did mean he should have been embrac'd:
But thou art fled. What hope is left for me?
I'll run to *Daphnis* in the hollow tree,
Whom I did mean to mock, though hope be small,
To make him bold; rather than none at all,
I'll try him; his heart, and my behaviour too
Perhaps may teach him what he ought to do.   [*Exit.*

Enter Sullen Shepherd.

Sul. This was the place, 'twas but my feeble sight,
Mixt with the horrour of my deed, and night,
That shap't these fears, and made me run away,
And lose my beauteous hardly gotten prey.
Speak gentle Shepherdess, I am alone,
And tender love for love: but she is gone
From me, that having struck her Lover dead,
For silly fear left her alone and fled.
And see the wounded body is remov'd
By her of whom it was so well belov'd.

The Faithful Shepherdess

Enter Perigot *and* Amaryllis *in the shape of* Amoret.

But these fancies must be quite forgot,
I must lye close. Here comes young *Perigot*
With subtile *Amaryllis* in the shape
Of *Amoret*. Pray Love he may not 'scape.

Amar. Beloved *Perigot*, shew me some place,
Where I may rest my limbs, weak with the Chace
Of thee, an hour before thou cam'st at least.

Per. Beshrew my tardy steps: here shalt thou rest
Upon this holy bank, no deadly Snake
Upon this turf her self in folds doth make.
Here is no poyson for the Toad to feed;
Here boldly spread thy hands, no venom'd Weed
Dares blister them, no slimy Snail dare creep
Over thy face when thou art fast asleep;
Here never durst the babling Cuckow spit,
No slough of falling Star did ever hit
Upon this bank: let this thy Cabin be,
This other set with Violets for me.

Ama. Thou dost not love me *Perigot*.

Per. Fair maid,
You only love to hear it often said;
You do not doubt.

Amar. Believe me but I do.

Per. What shall we now begin again to woo?
'Tis the best way to make your Lover last,
To play with him, when you have caught him fast.

Amar. By *Pan* I swear, I loved *Perigot*,
And by yon Moon, I think thou lov'st me not.

Per. By *Pan* I swear, and if I falsely swear,
Let him not guard my flocks, let Foxes tear
My earliest Lambs, and Wolves whilst I do sleep
Fall on the rest, a Rot among my Sheep.
I love thee better than the careful Ewe

The Faithful Shepherdess

The new-yean'd Lamb that is of her own hew;
I dote upon thee more than the young Lamb
Doth on the bag that feeds him from his Dam.
Were there a sort of Wolves got in my Fold,
And one ran after thee, both young and old
Should be devour'd, and it should be my strife
To save thee, whom I love above my life.

Ama. How shall I trust thee when I see thee chuse
Another Bed, and dost my side refuse?

Per. 'Twas only that the chast thoughts might be shewn
'Twixt thee and me, although we were alone.

Ama. Come, *Perigot* will shew his power, that he
Can make his *Amoret*, though she weary be,
Rise nimbly from her Couch, and come to his.
Here take thy *Amoret*, embrace and kiss.

Per. What means my Love?

Ama. To do as lovers shou'd,
That are to be enjoy'd, not to be woo'd.
There's ne'r a Shepherdess in all the plain
Can kiss thee with more Art, there's none can feign
More wanton tricks.

Per. Forbear, dear Soul, to trie
Whether my Heart be pure; I'll rather die
Than nourish one thought to dishonour thee.

Amar. Still think'st thou such a thing as Chastitie
Is amongst Women? *Perigot* there's none,
That with her Love is in a Wood alone,
And would come home a maid; be not abus'd
With thy fond first Belief, let time be us'd:
Why dost thou rise?

Per. My true heart thou hast slain.

Ama. Faith *Perigot*, I'll pluck thee down again.

Per. Let go, thou Serpent, that into my brest

Hast with thy cunning div'd; art not in Jest?

Ama. Sweet love, lye down.

Per. Since this I live to see,
Some bitter North-wind blast my flocks and me.

Ama. You swore you lov'd, yet will not do my will.

Per. O be as thou wert once, I'll love thee still.

Ama. I am, as still I was, and all my kind,
Though other shows we have poor men to blind.

Per. Then here I end all Love, and lest my vain
Belief should ever draw me in again,
Before thy face that hast my Youth misled,
I end my life, my blood be on thy head.

Ama. O hold thy hands, thy *Amoret* doth cry.

Per. Thou counsel'st well, first *Amoret* shall dye,
That is the cause of my eternal smart.   [*He runs after her.*

Ama. O hold.

Per. This steel shall pierce thy lustful heart.

[*The Sullen Shepherd steps out and uncharms her.*

Sull. Up and down every where,
I strew the herbs to purge the air:
Let your Odour drive hence
All mists that dazel sence.
Herbs and Springs whose hidden might
Alters Shapes, and mocks the sight,
Thus I charge you to undo
All before I brought ye to:
Let her flye, let her 'scape,
Give again her own shape.

Enter Amaryllis *in her own shape.*

Amar. Forbear thou gentle Swain, thou dost mistake,
She whom thou follow'dst fled into the brake,
And as I crost thy way, I met thy wrath,
The only fear of which near slain me hath.

Per. Pardon fair Shepherdess, my rage and night
Were both upon me, and beguil'd my sight;
But far be it from me to spill the blood
Of harmless Maids that wander in the Wood.   [*Ex.* Ama.

Enter Amoret.

Amor. Many a weary step in yonder path
Poor hopeless *Amoret* twice trodden hath
To seek her *Perigot*, yet cannot hear
His Voice; my *Perigot*, she loves thee dear
That calls.

Per. See yonder where she is, how fair
She shows, and yet her breath infefts the air.

Amo. My Perigot.

Per. Here.

Amo. Happy.

Per. Hapless first:
It lights on thee, the next blow is the worst.

Amo. Stay *Perigot*, my love, thou art unjust.

Peri. Death is the best reward that's due to lust.   [*Exit* Perigot.

Sul. Now shall their love be crost, for being struck,
I'le throw her in the Fount, lest being took
By some night-travaller, whose honest care
May help to cure her. Shepherdess prepare
Your self to die.

Amo. No Mercy I do crave,
Thou canst not give a worse blow than I have;
Tell him that gave me this, who lov'd him too,

He struck my soul, and not my body through,
Tell him when I am dead, my soul shall be
At peace, if he but think he injur'd me.

Sul. In this Fount be thy grave, thou wert not meant
Sure for a woman, thou art so innocent.   [*flings her into the well*
She cannot scape, for underneath the ground,
In a long hollow the clear spring is bound,
Till on yon side where the Morns Sun doth look,
The strugling water breaks out in a Brook.   [*Exit.*

[*The God of the River riseth with* Amoret *in his arms.*

God. What powerfull charms my streams do bring
Back again unto their spring,
With such force, that I their god,
Three times striking with my Rod,
Could not keep them in their ranks:
My Fishes shoot into the banks,
There's not one that stayes and feeds,
All have hid them in the weeds.
Here's a mortal almost dead,
Faln into my River head,
Hallowed so with many a spell,
That till now none ever fell.
'Tis a Female young and clear,
Cast in by some Ravisher.
See upon her breast a wound,
On which there is no plaister bound.
Yet she's warm, her pulses beat,
'Tis a sign of life and heat.
If thou be'st a Virgin pure,
I can give a present cure:
Take a drop into thy wound
From my watry locks more round
Than Orient Pearl, and far more pure
Than unchast flesh may endure.
See she pants, and from her flesh
The warm blood gusheth out afresh.
She is an unpolluted maid;
I must have this bleeding staid.
From my banks I pluck this flower
With holy hand, whose vertuous power

Is at once to heal and draw.
The blood returns. I never saw
A fairer Mortal. Now doth break
Her deadly slumber: Virgin, speak.

Amo. Who hath restor'd my sense, given me new breath,
And brought me back out of the arms of death?

God. I have heal'd thy wounds.

Amo. Ay me!

God. Fear not him that succour'd thee:
I am this Fountains god; below,
My waters to a River grow,
And 'twixt two banks with Osiers set,
That only prosper in the wet,
Through the Meadows do they glide,
Wheeling still on every side,
Sometimes winding round about,
To find the evenest channel out.
And if thou wilt go with me,
Leaving mortal companie,
In the cool streams shalt thou lye,
Free from harm as well as I:
I will give thee for thy food,
No Fish that useth in the mud,
But Trout and Pike that love to swim
Where the gravel from the brim
Through the pure streams may be seen:
Orient Pearl fit for a Queen,
Will I give thy love to win,
And a shell to keep them in:
Not a Fish in all my Brook
That shall disobey thy look,
But when thou wilt, come sliding by,
And from thy white hand take a fly.
And to make thee understand,
How I can my waves command,
They shall bubble whilst I sing
Sweeter than the silver spring.

The Faithful Shepherdess

The SONG.

Do not fear to put thy feet
Naked in the River sweet;
Think not Leach, or Newt or Toad
Will bite thy foot, when thou hast troad;
Nor let the water rising high,
As thou wad'st in, make thee crie
And sob, but ever live with me,
And not a wave shall trouble thee.

Amo. Immortal power, that rul'st this holy flood,
I know my self unworthy to be woo'd
By thee a god: for e're this, but for thee
I should have shown my weak Mortalitie:
Besides, by holy Oath betwixt us twain,
I am betroath'd unto a Shepherd swain,
Whose comely face, I know the gods above
May make me leave to see, but not to love.

God. May he prove to thee as true.
Fairest Virgin, now adieu,
I must make my waters fly,
Lest they leave their Channels dry,
And beasts that come unto the spring
Miss their mornings watering,
Which I would not; for of late
All the neighbour people sate
On my banks, and from the fold,
Two white Lambs of three weeks old
Offered to my Deitie:
For which this year they shall be free
From raging floods, that as they pass
Leave their gravel in the grass:
Nor shall their Meads be overflown,
When their grass is newly mown.

Amo. For thy kindness to me shown,
Never from thy banks be blown
Any tree, with windy force,
Cross thy streams, to stop thy course:
May no beast that comes to drink,
With his horns cast down thy brink;

May none that for thy fish do look,
Cut thy banks to damm thy Brook;
Bare-foot may no Neighbour wade
In thy cool streams, wife nor maid,
When the spawns on stones do lye,
To wash their Hemp, and spoil the Fry.

God. Thanks Virgin, I must down again,
Thy wound will put thee to no pain:
Wonder not so soon 'tis gone:
A holy hand was laid upon.

Amo. And I unhappy born to be,
Must follow him that flies from me.

The Faithful Shepherdess

Actus Quartus. Scena Prima.

Enter Perigot.

Per. She is untrue, unconstant, and unkind,
She's gone, she's gone, blow high thou North-west wind,
And raise the Sea to Mountains, let the Trees
That dare oppose thy raging fury, leese
Their firm foundation, creep into the Earth,
And shake the world, as at the monstrous birth
Of some new Prodigy, whilst I constant stand,
Holding this trustie Boar-spear in my hand,
And falling thus upon it.

Enter Amaryllis, *running.*

Amar. Stay thy dead-doing hand, thou art too hot
Against thy self, believe me comely Swain,
If that thou dyest, not all the showers of Rain
The heavy clods send down can wash away
That foul unmanly guilt, the world will lay
Upon thee. Yet thy love untainted stands:
Believe me, she is constant, not the sands
Can be so hardly numbred as she won:
I do not trifle, *Shepherd*, by the Moon,
And all those lesser lights our eyes do view,
All that I told thee *Perigot*, is true:
Then be a free man, put away despair,
And will to dye, smooth gently up that fair
Dejected forehead: be as when those eyes
Took the first heat.

Per. Alas he double dyes,
That would believe, but cannot; 'tis not well
Ye keep me thus from dying, here to dwell
With many worse companions: but oh death,
I am not yet inamour'd of this breath
So much, but I dare leave it, 'tis not pain
In forcing of a wound, nor after gain
Of many dayes, can hold me from my will:
'Tis not my self, but *Amoret*, bids kill.

Ama. Stay but a little, little, but one hour,
And if I do not show thee through the power
Of herbs and words I have, as dark as night,
My self turn'd to thy *Amoret*, in sight,
Her very figure, and the Robe she wears,
With tawny Buskins, and the hook she bears
Of thine own Carving, where your names are set,
Wrought underneath with many a curious fret,
The *Prim-Rose* Chaplet, taudry-lace and Ring,
Thou gavest her for her singing, with each thing
Else that she wears about her, let me feel
The first fell stroke of that Revenging steel.

Per. I am contented, if there be a hope
To give it entertainment, for the scope
Of one poor hour; goe, you shall find me next
Under yon shady Beech, even thus perplext,
And thus believing.

Ama. Bind before I goe,
Thy soul by *Pan* unto me, not to doe
Harm or outragious wrong upon thy life,
Till my return.

Per. By *Pan*, and by the strife
He had with *Phoebus* for the Mastery,
When Golden *Midas* judg'd their *Minstrelcy*,
I will not.   [*Exeunt.*

Enter Satyr, *with* Alexis, *hurt.*

Satyr. Softly gliding as I goe,
With this burthen full of woe,
Through still silence of the night,
Guided by the Gloe-worms light,
Hither am I come at last,
Many a Thicket have I past
Not a twig that durst deny me,
Not a bush that durst descry me,
To the little Bird that sleeps
On the tender spray: nor creeps
That hardy worm with pointed tail,
But if I be under sail,

45

Flying faster than the wind,
Leaving all the clouds behind,
But doth hide her tender head
In some hollow tree or bed
Of seeded Nettles: not a Hare
Can be started from his fare,
By my footing, nor a wish
Is more sudden, nor a fish
Can be found with greater ease,
Cut the vast unbounded seas,
Leaving neither print nor sound,
Than I, when nimbly on the ground,
I measure many a league an hour:
But behold the happy power,
That must ease me of my charge,
And by holy hand enlarge
The soul of this sad man, that yet
Lyes fast bound in deadly fit;
Heaven and great *Pan* succour it!
Hail thou beauty of the bower,
Whiter than the Paramour
Of my Master, let me crave
Thy vertuous help to keep from Grave
This poor Mortal that here lyes,
Waiting when the destinies
Will cut off his thred of life:
View the wound by cruel knife
Trencht into him.

Clor. What art thou call'st me from my holy rites,
And with thy feared name of death affrights
My tender Ears? speak me thy name and will.

Satyr. I am the *Satyr* that did fill
Your lap with early fruit, and will,
When I hap to gather more,
Bring ye better and more store:
Yet I come not empty now,
See a blossom from the bow,
But beshrew his heart that pull'd it,
And his perfect sight that cull'd it
From the other springing blooms;
For a sweeter youth the Grooms

Cannot show me, nor the downs,
Nor the many neighbouring towns;
Low in yonder glade I found him,
Softly in mine Arms I bound him,
Hither have I brought him sleeping
In a trance, his wounds fresh weeping,
In remembrance such youth may
Spring and perish in a day.

Clor. Satyr, they wrong thee, that do term thee rude,
Though thou beest outward rough and tawny hu'd,
Thy manners are as gentle and as fair
As his, who brags himself, born only heir
To all Humanity: let me see the wound:
This Herb will stay the current being bound
Fast to the Orifice, and this restrain
Ulcers, and swellings, and such inward pain,
As the cold air hath forc'd into the sore:
This to draw out such putrifying gore
As inward falls.

Satyr. Heaven grant it may doe good.

Clor. Fairly wipe away the blood:
Hold him gently till I fling
Water of a vertuous spring
On his temples; turn him twice
To the Moon beams, pinch him thrice,
That the labouring soul may draw
From his great eclipse.

Satyr. I saw
His eye-lids moving.

Clo. Give him breath,
All the danger of cold death
Now is vanisht; with this Plaster,
And this unction, do I master
All the festred ill that may
Give him grief another day.

Satyr. See he gathers up his spright
And begins to hunt for light;

47

The Faithful Shepherdess

Now he gapes and breaths again:
How the blood runs to the vein,
That erst was empty!

Alex. O my heart,
My dearest, dearest *Cloe*, O the smart
Runs through my side: I feel some pointed thing
Pass through my Bowels, sharper than the sting
Of Scorpion.

Pan preserve me, what are you?
Do not hurt me, I am true
To my *Cloe*, though she flye,
And leave me to thy destiny.
There she stands, and will not lend
Her smooth white hand to help her friend:

But I am much mistaken, for that face
Bears more Austerity and modest grace,

More reproving and more awe
Than these eyes yet ever saw
In my Cloe. Oh my pain
Eagerly renews again.

Give me your help for his sake you love best.

Clor. Shepherd, thou canst not possibly take rest,
Till thou hast laid aside all hearts desires
Provoking thought that stir up lusty fires,
Commerce with wanton eyes, strong blood, and will
To execute, these must be purg'd, untill
The vein grow whiter; then repent, and pray
Great *Pan* to keep you from the like decay,
And I shall undertake your cure with ease.
Till when this vertuous Plaster will displease
Your tender sides; give me your hand and rise:
Help him a little *Satyr*, for his thighs
Yet are feeble.

Alex. Sure I have lost much blood.

Satyr. 'Tis no matter, 'twas not good.

Mortal you must leave your wooing,
Though there be a joy in doing,
Yet it brings much grief behind it,
They best feel it, that do find it.

Clor. Come bring him in, I will attend his sore
When you are well, take heed you lust no more.

Satyr. Shepherd, see what comes of kissing,
By my head 'twere better missing.
Brightest, if there be remaining
Any service, without feigning
I will do it; were I set
To catch the nimble wind, or get
Shadows gliding on the green,
Or to steal from the great Queen
Of *Fayries,* all her beauty,
I would do it, so much duty
Do I owe those precious Eyes.

Clor. I thank thee honest *Satyr,* if the cryes
Of any other that be hurt or ill,
Draw thee unto them, prithee do thy will
To bring them hither.

Satyr. I will, and when the weather
Serves to Angle in the brook,
I will bring a silver hook,
With a line of finest silk,
And a rod as white as milk,
To deceive the little fish:
So I take my leave, and wish,
On this Bower may ever dwell
Spring, and Summer.

Clo. Friend farewel.   [*Exit.*

Enter Amoret, *seeking her Love.*

Amor. This place is Ominous, for here I lost
My Love and almost life, and since have crost
All these Woods over, never a Nook or Dell,
Where any little Bird, or Beast doth dwell,

But I have sought him, never a bending brow
Of any Hill or Glade, the wind sings through,
Nor a green bank, nor shade where Shepherds use
To sit and Riddle, sweetly pipe, or chuse
Their Valentines, that I have mist, to find
My love in. *Perigot*, Oh too unkind,
Why hast thou fled me? whither art thou gone?
How have I wrong'd thee? was my love alone
To thee worthy this scorn'd recompence? 'tis well,
I am content to feel it: but I tell
Thee Shepherd, and these lusty woods shall hear,
Forsaken *Amoret* is yet as clear
Of any stranger fire, as Heaven is
From foul corruption, or the deep Abysse
From light and happiness; and thou mayst know
All this for truth, and how that fatal blow
Thou gav'st me, never from desert of mine,
Fell on my life, but from suspect of thine,
Or fury more than madness; therefore, here,
Since I have lost my life, my love, my dear,
Upon this cursed place, and on this green,
That first divorc'd us, shortly shall be seen
A sight of so great pity, that each eye
Shall dayly spend his spring in memory
Of my untimely fall.

Enter Amaryllis.

Amar. I am not blind,
Nor is it through the working of my mind,
That this shows *Amoret*; forsake me all
That dwell upon the soul, but what men call
Wonder, or more than wonder, miracle,
For sure so strange as this the Oracle
Never gave answer of, it passeth dreams,
Or mad-mens fancy, when the many streams
Of new imaginations rise and fall:
'Tis but an hour since these Ears heard her call
For pity to young *Perigot*; whilest he,
Directed by his fury bloodily
Lanc't up her brest, which bloodless fell and cold;
And if belief may credit what was told,
After all this, the Melancholy Swain

Took her into his arms being almost slain,
And to the bottom of the holy well
Flung her, for ever with the waves to dwell.
'Tis she, the very same, 'tis *Amoret*,
And living yet, the great powers will not let
Their vertuous love be crost. Maid, wipe away
Those heavy drops of sorrow, and allay
The storm that yet goes high, which not deprest,
Breaks heart and life, and all before it rest:
Thy *Perigot* —

Amor. Where, which is *Perigot?*

Amar. Sits there below, lamenting much, god wot,
Thee [and thy] fortune, go and comfort him,
And thou shalt find him underneath a brim
Of sailing Pines that edge yon Mountain in.

Amo. I go, I run, Heaven grant me I may win
His soul again. [*Exit* Amoret.

Enter Sullen.

Sull. Stay *Amaryllis*, stay,
Ye are too fleet, 'tis two hours yet to day.
I have perform'd my promise, let us sit
And warm our bloods together till the fit
Come lively on us.

Amar. Friend you are too keen,
The morning riseth and we shall be seen,
Forbear a little.

Sull. I can stay no longer.

Amar. Hold *Shepherd* hold, learn not to be a wronger
Of your word, was not your promise laid,
To break their loves first?

Sull. I have done it Maid.

Amar. No, they are yet unbroken, met again,
And are as hard to part yet as the stain

51

Is from the finest Lawn.

Sull. I say they are
Now at this present parted, and so far,
That they shall never meet.

Amar. Swain 'tis not so,
For do but to yon hanging Mountain go,
And there believe your eyes.

Sull. You do but hold
Off with delayes and trifles; farewell cold
And frozen bashfulness, unfit for men;
Thus I salute thee Virgin.

Amar. And thus then,
I bid you follow, catch me if you can.   [*Exit.*

Sull. And if I stay behind I am no man.   [*Exit running after her.*

Enter Perigot.

Per. Night do not steal away: I woo thee yet
To hold a hard hand o're the rusty bit
That guides the lazy Team: go back again,
Bootes, thou that driv'st thy frozen Wain
Round as a Ring, and bring a second Night
To hide my sorrows from the coming light;
Let not the eyes of men stare on my face,
And read my falling, give me some black place
Where never Sun-beam shot his wholesome light,
That I may sit and pour out my sad spright
Like running water, never to be known
After the forced fall and sound is gone.

Enter Amoret *looking for* Perigot.

Amo. This is the bottom: speak if thou be here,
My *Perigot*, thy *Amoret*, thy dear
Calls on thy loved Name.

Per. What art thou [dare]
Tread these forbidden paths, where death and care

Dwell on the face of darkness?

Amo. 'Tis thy friend,
Thy *Amoret*, come hither to give end
To these consumings; look up gentle Boy,
I have forgot those Pains and dear annoy
I suffer'd for thy sake, and am content
To be thy love again; why hast thou rent
Those curled locks, where I have often hung
Riband and Damask-roses, and have flung
Waters distil'd to make thee fresh and gay,
Sweeter than the Nosegayes on a Bridal day?
Why dost thou cross thine Arms, and hang thy face
Down to thy bosom, letting fall apace
From those two little Heavens upon the ground
Showers of more price, more Orient, and more round
Than those that hang upon the Moons pale brow?
Cease these complainings, Shepherd, I am now
The same I ever was, as kind and free,
And can forgive before you ask of me.
Indeed I can and will.

Per. So spoke my fair.
O you great working powers of Earth and Air,
Water and forming fire, why have you lent
Your hidden vertues of so ill intent?
Even such a face, so fair, so bright of hue
Had *Amoret*; such words so smooth and new,
Came flying from her tongue; such was her eye,
And such the pointed sparkle that did flye
Forth like a bleeding shaft; all is the same,
The Robe and Buskins, painted Hook, and frame
Of all her Body. O me, *Amoret*!

Amo. Shepherd, what means this Riddle? who hath set
So strong a difference 'twixt my self and me
That I am grown another? look and see
The Ring thou gav'st me, and about my wrist
That curious Bracelet thou thy self didst twist
From those fair Tresses: knowst thou *Amoret*?
Hath not some newer love forc'd thee forget
Thy Ancient faith?

Per. Still nearer to my love;
These be the very words she oft did prove
Upon my temper, so she still would take
Wonder into her face, and silent make
Signs with her head and hand, as who would say,
Shepherd remember this another day.

Amo. Am I not *Amaret*? where was I lost?
Can there be Heaven, and time, and men, and most
Of these unconstant? Faith where art thou fled?
Are all the vows and protestations dead,
The hands [held] up, the wishes, and the heart,
Is there not one remaining, not a part
Of all these to be found? why then I see
Men never knew that vertue Constancie.

Per. Men ever were most blessed, till crass fate
Brought Love and Women forth, unfortunate
To all that ever tasted of their smiles,
Whose actions are all double, full of wiles:
Like to the subtil Hare, that 'fore the Hounds
Makes many turnings, leaps and many rounds,
This way and that way, to deceive the scent
Of her pursuers.

Amo. 'Tis but to prevent
Their speedy coming on that seek her fall,
The hands of cruel men, more Bestial,
And of a nature more refusing good
Than Beasts themselves, or Fishes of the Flood.

Per. Thou art all these, and more than nature meant,
When she created all, frowns, joys, content;
Extream fire for an hour, and presently
Colder than sleepy poyson, or the Sea,
Upon whose face sits a continual frost:
Your actions ever driven to the most,
Then down again as low, that none can find
The rise or falling of a Womans mind.

Amo. Can there be any Age, or dayes, or time,
Or tongues of men, guilty so great a crime
As wronging simple Maid? O *Perigot*,

The Faithful Shepherdess

Thou that wast yesterday without a blot,
Thou that wast every good, and every thing
That men call blessed; thou that wast the spring
From whence our looser grooms drew all their best;
Thou that wast always just, and alwayes blest
In faith and promise; thou that hadst the name
Of Vertuous given thee, and made good the same
Ev'en from thy Cradle; thou that wast that all
That men delighted in; Oh what a fall
Is this, to have been so, and now to be
The only best in wrong and infamie,
And I to live to know this! and by me
That lov'd thee dearer than mine eyes, or that
Which we esteem'd our honour, Virgin state;
Dearer than Swallows love the early morn,
Or Dogs of Chace the sound of merry Horn;
Dearer than thou canst love thy new Love, if thou hast
Another, and far dearer than the last;
Dearer than thou canst love thy self, though all
The self love were within thee that did fall
With that coy Swain that now is made a flower,
For whose dear sake, Echo weeps many a shower.
And am I thus rewarded for my flame?
Lov'd worthily to get a wantons name?
Come thou forsaken Willow, wind my head,
And noise it to the world my Love is dead:
I am forsaken, I am cast away.
And left for every lazy Groom to say,
I was unconstant, light, and sooner lost
Than the quick Clouds we see, or the chill Frost
When the hot Sun beats on it. Tell me yet,
Canst thou not love again thy *Amoret*?

Per. Thou art not worthy of that blessed name,
I must not know thee, fling thy wanton flame
Upon some lighter blood, that may be hot
With words and feigned passions: *Perigot*
Was ever yet unstain'd, and shall not now
Stoop to the meltings of a borrowed brow.

Amo. Then hear me heaven, to whom I call for right,
And you fair twinkling stars that crown the night;
And hear me woods, and silence of this place,

And ye sad hours that move a sullen pace;
Hear me ye shadows that delight to dwell
In horrid darkness, and ye powers of Hell,
Whilst I breath out my last; I am that maid,
That yet untainted *Amoret*, that plaid
The careless prodigal, and gave away
My soul to this young man, that now dares say
I am a stranger, not the same, more wild;
And thus with much belief I was beguil'd.
I am that maid, that have delaid, deny'd,
And almost scorn'd the loves of all that try'd
To win me, but this swain, and yet confess
I have been woo'd by many with no less
Soul of affection, and have often had
Rings, Belts, and Cracknels sent me from the lad
That feeds his flocks down westward; Lambs and Doves
By young *Alexis; Daphnis* sent me gloves,
All which I gave to thee: nor these, nor they
That sent them did I smile on, or e're lay
Up to my after-memory. But why
Do I resolve to grieve, and not to dye?
Happy had been the stroke thou gav'st, if home;
By this time had I found a quiet room
Where every slave is free, and every brest
That living breeds new care, now lies at rest,
And thither will poor *Amoret*.

Per. Thou must.
Was ever any man so loth to trust
His eyes as I? or was there ever yet
Any so like as this to *Amoret*?
For whose dear sake, I promise if there be
A living soul within thee, thus to free
Thy body from it.   [*He hurts her again.*

Amo. So, this work hath end:
Farewel and live, be constant to thy friend
That loves thee next.

Enter Satyr, Perigot *runs off.*

Satyr. See the day begins to break,
And the light shoots like a streak

56

Of subtil fire, the wind blows cold,
Whilst the morning doth unfold;
Now the Birds begin to rouse,
And the Squirril from the boughs
Leaps to get him Nuts and fruit;
The early Lark that erst was mute,
Carrols to the rising day
Many a note and many a lay:
Therefore here I end my watch,
Lest the wandring swain should catch
Harm, or lose himself.

Amo. Ah me!

Satyr. Speak again what e're thou be,
I am ready, speak I say:
By the dawning of the day,
By the power of night and *Pan*,
I inforce thee speak again.

Amo. O I am most unhappy.

Satyr. Yet more blood!
Sure these wanton Swains are wode.
Can there be a hand or heart
Dare commit so vile a part
As this Murther? By the Moon
That hid her self when this was done,
Never was a sweeter face:
I will bear her to the place
Where my Goddess keeps; and crave
Her to give her life, or grave.   [*Exeunt.*

Enter Clorin.

Clor. Here whilst one patient takes his rest secure
I steal abroad to doe another Cure.
Pardon thou buryed body of my love,
That from thy side I dare so soon remove,
I will not prove unconstant, nor will leave
Thee for an hour alone. When I deceive
My first made vow, the wildest of the wood
Tear me, and o're thy Grave let out my blood;

57

I goe by wit to cure a lovers pain
Which no herb can; being done, I'le come again.   [*Exit.*

Enter Thenot.

The. Poor Shepherd in this shade for ever lye,
And seeing thy fair *Clorins* Cabin, dye:
0 hapless love, which [being] answer'd, ends;
And as a little infant cryes and bends
His tender Brows, when rowling of his eye
He hath espy'd some thing that glisters nigh
Which he would have, yet give it him, away
He throws it straight, and cryes afresh to play
With something else: such my affection, set
On that which I should loath, if I could get.

Enter Clorin.

Clor. See where he lyes; did ever man but he
Love any woman for her Constancie
To her dead lover, which she needs must end
Before she can allow him for her friend,
And he himself must needs the cause destroy,
For which he loves, before he can enjoy?
Poor *Shepherd*, Heaven grant I at once may free
Thee from thy pain, and keep my loyaltie:
Shepherd, look up.

The. Thy brightness doth amaze!
So *Phoebus* may at noon bid mortals gaze,
Thy glorious constancie appears so bright,
I dare not meet the Beams with my weak sight.

Clor. Why dost thou pine away thy self for me?

The. Why dost thou keep such spotless constancie?

Clor. Thou holy *Shepherd*, see what for thy sake
Clorin, thy *Clorin*, now dare under take.   [*He starts up.*

The. Stay there, thou constant *Clorin*, if there be
Yet any part of woman left in thee,
To make thee light: think yet before thou speak.

Clor. See what a holy vow for thee I break.
I that already have my fame far spread
For being constant to my lover dead.

The. Think yet, dear *Clorin*, of your love, how true,
If you had dyed, he would have been to you.

Clor. Yet all I'le lose for thee.

The. Think but how blest
A constant woman is above the rest.

Clor. And offer up my self, here on this ground,
To be dispos'd by thee.

The. Why dost thou wound
His heart with malice, against woman more,
That hated all the Sex, but thee before?
How much more pleasant had it been to me
To dye, than to behold this change in thee?
Yet, yet, return, let not the woman sway.

Clor. Insult not on her now, nor use delay,
Who for thy sake hath ventur'd all her fame.

The. Thou hast not ventur'd, but bought certain shame,
Your Sexes curse, foul falshood must and shall,
I see, once in your lives, light on you all.
I hate thee now: yet turn.

Clor. Be just to me:
Shall I at once both lose my fame and thee?

The. Thou hadst no fame, that which thou didst like good,
Was but thy appetite that sway'd thy blood
For that time to the best: for as a blast
That through a house comes, usually doth cast
Things out of order, yet by chance may come,
And blow some one thing to his proper room;
So did thy appetite, and not thy zeal,
Sway thee [by] chance to doe some one thing well.
Yet turn.

The Faithful Shepherdess

Clor. Thou dost but try me if I would
Forsake thy dear imbraces, for my old
Love's, though he were alive: but do not fear.

The. I do contemn thee now, and dare come near,
And gaze upon thee; for me thinks that grace,
Austeritie, which sate upon that face
Is gone, and thou like others: false maid see,
This is the gain of foul inconstancie.   [*Exit.*

Clor. 'Tis done, great *Pan* I give thee thanks for it,
What art could not have heal'd, is cur'd by wit.

Enter Thenot, *again.*

The. Will ye be constant yet? will ye remove
Into the Cabin to your buried Love?

Clor. No let me die, but by thy side remain.

The. There's none shall know that thou didst ever stain
Thy worthy strictness, but shall honour'd be,
And I will lye again under this tree,
And pine and dye for thee with more delight,
Than I have sorrow now to know the light.

Clor. Let me have thee, and I'le be where thou wilt.

The. Thou art of womens race, and full of guilt.
Farewel all hope of that Sex, whilst I thought
There was one good, I fear'd to find one naught:
But since their minds I all alike espie,
Henceforth I'le choose as others, by mine eye.

Clor. Blest be ye powers that give such quick redress,
And for my labours sent so good success.
I rather choose, though I a woman be,
He should speak ill of all, than die for me.

The Faithful Shepherdess

Actus Quintus. Scena Prima.

Enter Priest, *and old* Shepherd.

Priest. Shepherds, rise and shake off sleep,
See the blushing Morn doth peep
Through the window, whilst the Sun
To the mountain tops is run,
Gilding all the Vales below
With his rising flames, which grow
Greater by his climbing still.
Up ye lazie grooms, and fill
Bagg and Bottle for the field;
Clasp your cloaks fast, lest they yield
To the bitter North-east wind.
Call the Maidens up, and find
Who lay longest, that she may
Goe without a friend all day;
Then reward your Dogs, and pray
Pan to keep you from decay:
So unfold and then away.
What not a Shepherd stirring? sure the grooms
Have found their beds too easie, or the rooms
Fill'd with such new delight, and heat, that they
Have both forgot their hungry sheep, and day;
Knock, that they may remember what a shame
Sloath and neglect layes on a Shepherds name.

Old Shep. It is to little purpose, not a swain
This night hath known his lodging here, or lain
Within these cotes: the woods, or some near town,
That is a neighbour to the bordering Down,
Hath drawn them thither, 'bout some lustie sport,
Or spiced Wassel-Boul, to which resort
All the young men and maids of many a cote,
Whilst the trim Minstrel strikes his merry note.

Priest. God pardon sin, show me the way that leads
To any of their haunts.

Old Shep. This to the meads,
And that down to the woods.

The Faithful Shepherdess

Priest. Then this for me;
Come Shepherd let me crave your companie.   [*Exeunt.*

Enter Clorin, *in her Cabin,* Alexis, *with her.*

Clor. Now your thoughts are almost pure,
And your wound begins to cure:
Strive to banish all that's vain,
Lest it should break out again.

Alex. Eternal thanks to thee, thou holy maid:
I find my former wandring thoughts well staid
Through thy wise precepts, and my outward pain
By thy choice herbs is almost gone again:
Thy sexes vice and vertue are reveal'd
At once, for what one hurt, another heal'd.

Clor. May thy grief more appease,
Relapses are the worst disease.
Take heed how you in thought offend,
So mind and body both will mend.

Enter Satyr, *with* Amoret.

Amo. Beest thou the wildest creature of the wood,
That bearst me thus away, drown'd in my blood,
And dying, know I cannot injur'd be,
I am a maid, let that name fight for me.

Satyr. Fairest Virgin do not fear
Me, that do thy body bear,
Not to hurt, but heal'd to be;
Men are ruder far than we.
See fair *Goddess* in the wood,
They have let out yet more blood.
Some savage man hath struck her breast
So soft and white, that no wild beast
Durst ha' toucht asleep, or wake:
So sweet, that *Adder, Newte,* or *Snake,*
Would have lain from arm to arm,
On her bosom to be warm
All a night, and being hot,
Gone away and stung her not.

The Faithful Shepherdess

Quickly clap herbs to her breast;
A man sure is a kind of beast.

Clor. With spotless hand, on spotless brest
I put these herbs to give thee rest:
Which till it heal thee, will abide,
If both be pure, if not, off slide.
See it falls off from the wound,
Shepherdess thou art not sound,
Full of lust.

Only heal pure

Satyr, Who would have thought it,
So fair a face?

Clor. Why that hath brought it.

Amo. For ought I know or think, these words, my last:
Yet *Pan* so help me as my thoughts are chast.

Clor. And so may *Pan* bless this my cure,
As all my thoughts are just and pure;
Some uncleanness nigh doth lurk,
That will not let my Medicines work.
Satyr search if thou canst find it.

Satyr. Here away methinks I wind it,
Stronger yet: Oh here they be,
Here, here, in a hollow tree,
Two fond mortals have I found.

Clor. Bring them out, they are unsound.

Enter Cloe, *and* Daphnis.

Satyr. By the fingers thus I wring ye,
To my *Goddess* thus I bring ye;
Strife is vain, come gently in,
I scented them, they're full of sin.

Clor. Hold *Satyr,* take this Glass,
Sprinkle over all the place,
Purge the Air from lustfull breath,
To save this Shepherdess from death,

And stand you still whilst I do dress
Her wound for fear the pain encrease.

Sat. From this glass I throw a drop
Of Crystal water on the top
Of every grass, on flowers a pair:
Send a fume and keep the air
Pure and wholsom, sweet and blest,
Till this Virgins wound be drest.

Clor. Satyr, help to bring her in.

Sat. By *Pan*, I think she hath no sin,
She is so light: lye on these leaves.
Sleep that mortal sense deceives,
Crown thine Eyes, and ease thy pain,
Maist thou soon be well again.

Clor. Satyr, bring the Shepherd near,
Try him if his mind be clear.

Sat. Shepherd come.

Daph. My thoughts are pure.

Sat. The better trial to endure.

Clor. In this flame his finger thrust,
Which will burn him if he lust;
But if not, away will turn,
As loth unspotted flesh to burn:
See, it gives back, let him go,
Farewel mortal, keep thee so.

Sat. Stay fair *Nymph*, flye not so fast,
We must try if you be chaste:
Here's a hand that quakes for fear,
Sure she will not prove so clear.

Clor. Hold her finger to the flame,
That will yield her praise or shame.

Sat. To her doom she dares not stand,

But plucks away her tender hand,
And the Taper darting sends
His hot beams at her fingers ends:
O thou art foul within, and hast
A mind, if nothing else, unchaste.

Alex. Is not that *Cloe?* 'tis my Love, 'tis she!
Cloe, fair *Cloe.*

Clo. My Alexis.

Alex. He.

Clo. Let me embrace thee.

Clor. Take her hence,
Lest her sight disturb his sence.

Alex. Take not her, take my life first.

Clor. See, his wound again is burst:
Keep her near, here in the Wood,
Till I ha' stopt these Streams of Blood.
Soon again he ease shall find,
If I can but still his mind:
This Curtain thus I do display,
To keep the piercing air away.

Enter old Shepherd, *and* Priest.

Priest. Sure they are lost for ever; 'tis in vain
To find 'em out with trouble and much pain,
That have a ripe desire, and forward will
To flye the Company of all but ill,
What shall be counsel'd now? shall we retire?
Or constant follow still that first desire
We had to find them?

Old. Stay a little while;
For if the Morning mist do not beguile
My sight with shadows, sure I see a Swain;
One of this jolly Troop's come back again.

The Faithful Shepherdess

Enter Thenot.

Pri. Dost thou not blush young Shepherd to be known,
Thus without care, leaving thy flocks alone,
And following what desire and present blood
Shapes out before thy burning sense, for good,
Having forgot what tongue hereafter may
Tell to the World thy falling off, and say
Thou art regardless both of good and shame,
Spurning at Vertue, and a vertuous Name,
And like a glorious, desperate man that buys
A poyson of much price, by which he dies,
Dost thou lay out for Lust, whose only gain
Is foul disease, with present age and pain,
And then a Grave? These be the fruits that grow
In such hot Veins that only beat to know
Where they may take most ease, and grow ambitious
Through their own wanton fire, and pride delicious.

The. Right holy Sir, I have not known this night,
What the smooth face of Mirth was, or the sight
Of any looseness; musick, joy, and ease,
Have been to me as bitter drugs to please
A Stomach lost with weakness, not a game
That I am skill'd at throughly; nor a Dame,
Went her tongue smoother than the feet of Time,
Her beauty ever living like the Rime
Our blessed *Tityrus* did sing of yore,
No, were she more enticing than the store
Of fruitful Summer, when the loaden Tree
Bids the faint Traveller be bold and free,
'Twere but to me like thunder 'gainst the bay,
Whose lightning may enclose but never stay
Upon his charmed branches; such am I
Against the catching flames of Womans eye.

Priest. Then wherefore hast thou wandred?

The. 'Twas a Vow
That drew me out last night, which I have now
Strictly perform'd, and homewards go to give
Fresh pasture to my Sheep, that they may live.

Pri. 'Tis good to hear ye, Shepherd, if the heart
In this well sounding Musick bear his part.
Where have you left the rest?

The. I have not seen,
Since yesternight we met upon this green
To fold our Flocks up, any of that train;
Yet have I walkt these Woods round, and have lain
All this same night under an aged Tree,
Yet neither wandring Shepherd did I see,
Or Shepherdess, or drew into mine ear
The sound of living thing, unless it were
The Nightingale among the thick leav'd spring
That sits alone in sorrow, and doth sing
Whole nights away in mourning, or the Owl,
Or our great enemy that still doth howl
Against the Moons cold beams.

Priest. Go and beware
Of after falling.

The. Father 'tis my care.   [*Exit* Thenot.

Enter Daphnis.

Old. Here comes another Stragler, sure I see
A Shame in this young Shepherd. *Daphnis!*

Daph. He.

Pri. Where hast thou left the rest, that should have been
Long before this, grazing upon the green
Their yet imprison'd flocks?

Daph. Thou holy man,
Give me a little breathing till I can
Be able to unfold what I have seen;
Such horrour that the like hath never been
Known to the ear of Shepherd: Oh my heart
Labours a double motion to impart
So heavy tidings! You all know the Bower
Where the chast *Clorin* lives, by whose great power
Sick men and Cattel have been often cur'd,

There lovely *Amoret* that was assur'd
To lusty *Perigot*, bleeds out her life,
Forc'd by some Iron hand and fatal knife;
And by her young *Alexis*.

Enter Amaryllis *running from her* Sullen Shepherd.

Amar. If there be
Ever a Neighbour Brook, or hollow tree,
Receive my Body, close me up from lust
That follows at my heels; be ever just,
Thou god of Shepherds, *Pan*, for her dear sake
That loves the Rivers brinks, and still doth shake
In cold remembrance of thy quick pursuit:
Let me be made a reed, and ever mute,
Nod to the waters fall, whilst every blast
Sings through my slender leaves that I was chast.

Pri. This is a night of wonder, *Amaryll*
Be comforted, the holy gods are still
Revengers of these wrongs.

Amar. Thou blessed man,
Honour'd upon these plains, and lov'd of *Pan*,
Hear me, and save from endless infamie
My yet unblasted Flower, *Virginitie*:
By all the Garlands that have crown'd that head,
By the chaste office, and the Marriage bed
That still is blest by thee, by all the rights
Due to our gods; and by those Virgin lights
That burn before his Altar, let me not
Fall from my former state to gain the blot
That never shall be purg'd: I am not now
That wanton *Amaryllis*: here I vow
To Heaven, and thee grave Father, if I may
'Scape this unhappy Night, to know the Day,
To live a Virgin, never to endure
The tongues, or Company of men impure.
I hear him come, save me.

Pri. Retire a while
Behind this Bush, till we have known that vile
Abuser of young Maidens.

The Faithful Shepherdess

Enter Sullen.

Sul. Stay thy pace,
Most loved *Amaryllis*, let the Chase
Grow calm and milder, flye me not so fast,
I fear the pointed Brambles have unlac'd
Thy golden Buskins; turn again and see
Thy Shepherd follow, that is strong and free,
Able to give thee all content and ease.
I am not bashful, Virgin, I can please
At first encounter, hug thee in mine arm,
And give thee many Kisses, soft and warm
As those the Sun prints on the smiling Cheek
Of Plums, or mellow Peaches; I am sleek
And smooth as *Neptune*, when stern *Eolus*
Locks up his surly Winds, and nimbly thus
Can shew my active Youth; why dost thou flye?
Remember *Amaryllis*, it was I
That kill'd *Alexis* for thy sake, and set
An everlasting hate 'twixt *Amoret*
And her beloved *Perigot*: 'twas I
That drown'd her in the Well, where she must lye
Till Time shall leave to be; then turn again,
Turn with thy open arms, and clip the Swain
That hath perform'd all this, turn, turn I say:
I must not be deluded.

Pri. Monster stay,
Thou that art like a Canker to the State
Thou liv'st and breath'st in, eating with debate
Through every honest bosome, forcing still
The Veins of any that may serve thy Will,
Thou that hast offer'd with a sinful hand
To seize upon this Virgin that doth stand
Yet trembling here.

Sull. Good holiness declare,
What had the danger been, if being bare
I had embrac'd her, tell me by your Art,
What coming wonders would that sight impart?

Pri. Lust, and a branded Soul.

Sull. Yet tell me more,
Hath not our Mother Nature for her store
And great encrease, said it is good and just,
And wills that every living Creature must
Beget his like?

Pri. Ye are better read than I,
I must confess, in blood and Lechery.
Now to the Bower, and bring this Beast along,
Where he may suffer Penance for his wrong.   [*Exeunt.*

Enter Perigot *with his hands bloody.*

Per. Here will I wash it in this mornings dew,
Which she on every little grass doth strew
In silver drops against the Sun's appear:
'Tis holy water, and will make me clear.
My hands will not be cleans'd. My wronged Love,
If thy chaste spirit in the air yet move,
Look mildly down on him that yet doth stand
All full of guilt, thy blood upon his hand,
And though I struck thee undeservedly,
Let my revenge on her that injur'd thee
Make less a fault which I intended not,
And let these dew drops wash away my spot.
It will not cleanse. O to what sacred Flood
Shall I resort to wash away this blood?
Amid'st these Trees the holy *Clorin* dwells
In a low Cabin of cut Boughs, and heals
All Wounds; to her I will my self address,
And my rash faults repentantly confess;
Perhaps she'll find a means by Art or Prayer,
To make my hand with chaste blood stained, fair:
That done, not far hence underneath some Tree,
I'll have a little Cabin built, since she
Whom I ador'd is dead, there will I give
My self to strictness, and like *Clorin* live.   [*Exit.*

The Curtain is drawn, Clorin *appears sitting in the Cabin,* Amoret
sitting on the one side of her, Alexis *and* Cloe *on the other, the*
Satyr *standing by.*

Clo. Shepherd, once more your blood is staid,

The Faithful Shepherdess

Take example by this Maid,
Who is heal'd ere you be pure,
So hard it is lewd lust to cure.
Take heed then how you turn your eye
On each other lustfully:
And Shepherdess take heed lest you
Move his willing eye thereto;
Let no wring, nor pinch, nor smile
Of yours his weaker sense beguile.
Is your Love yet true and chaste,
And for ever so to last?

Alex. I have forgot all vain desires,
All looser thoughts, ill tempred fires,
True Love I find a pleasant fume,
Whose moderate heat can ne'r consume.

Clo. And I a new fire feel in me,
Whose chaste flame is not quencht to be.

Clor. Join your hands with modest touch,
And for ever keep you such.

Enter Perigot.

Per. Yon is her Cabin, thus far off I'll stand,
And call her forth; for my unhallowed hand
I dare not bring so near yon sacred place.
Clorin come forth, and do a timely grace
To a poor Swain.

Clo. What art thou that dost call?
Clorin is ready to do good to all:
Come near.

Peri. I dare not.

Clor. Satyr, see
Who it is that calls on me.

Sat. There at hand, some Swain doth stand,
Stretching out a bloudy hand.

Peri. Come *Clorin*, bring thy holy waters clear,
To wash my hand.

Clo. What wonders have been here
To night? stretch forth thy hand young Swain,
Wash and rub it whilest I rain
Holy water.

Peri. Still you pour,
But my hand will never scower.

Clor. Satyr, bring him to the Bower,
We will try the Soveraign power
Of other waters.

Satyr. Mortal, sure
'Tis the Blood of Maiden pure
That stains thee so.

[*The* Satyr *leadeth him to the Bower, where he spieth* Amoret, *and kneeling down, she knoweth him.*

Peri. What e're thou be,
Be'st thou her spright, or some divinitie,
That in her shape thinks good to walk this grove,
Pardon poor *Perigot.*

Amor. I am thy love,
Thy *Amoret*, for evermore thy love:
Strike once more on my naked breast, I'le prove
As constant still. O couldst thou love me yet;
How soon should I my former griefs forget!

Peri. So over-great with joy, that you live, now
I am, that no desire of knowing how
Doth seize me; hast thou still power to forgive?

Amo. Whilest thou hast power to love, or I to live;
More welcome now than hadst thou never gone
Astray from me.

Peri. And when thou lov'st alone
And not I, death, or some lingring pain

That's worse, light on me.

Clor. Now your stain
This perhaps will cleanse again;
See the blood that erst did stay,
With the water drops away.
All the powers again are pleas'd,
And with this new knot appeas'd.
Joyn your hands, and rise together,
Pan be blest that brought you hither.

Enter Priest, *and* Old Shephe[rd].

Clor. Go back again what ere thou art, unless
Smooth Maiden thoughts possess thee, do not press
This hallowed ground. Go *Satyr*, take his hand,
And give him present trial.

Satyr. Mortal stand,
Till by fire I have made known
Whether thou be such a one,
That mayst freely tread this place.
Hold thy hand up; never was
More untainted flesh than this.
Fairest, he is full of bliss.

Clor. Then boldly speak, why dost thou seek this place?

Priest. First, honour'd Virgin, to behold thy face
Where all good dwells that is: Next for to try
The truth of late report was given to me:
Those Shepherds that have met with foul mischance,
Through much neglect, and more ill governance,
Whether the wounds they have may yet endure
The open Air, or stay a longer cure.
And lastly, what the doom may be shall light
Upon those guilty wretches, through whose spight
All this confusion fell: For to this place,
Thou holy Maiden, have I brought the race
Of these offenders, who have freely told,
Both why, and by what means they gave this bold
Attempt upon their lives.

Clor. Fume all the ground,
And sprinkle holy water, for unsound
And foul infection 'gins to fill the Air:
It gathers yet more strongly; take a pair
Of Censors fill'd with Frankincense and Mirrh,
Together with cold Camphyre: quickly stir
Thee, gentle *Satyr*, for the place begins
To sweat and labour with the abhorred sins
Of those offenders; let them not come nigh,
For full of itching flame and leprosie
Their very souls are, that the ground goes back,
And shrinks to feel the sullen weight of black
And so unheard of venome; hie thee fast
Thou holy man, and banish from the chast
These manlike monsters, let them never more
Be known upon these downs, but long before
The next Suns rising, put them from the sight
And memory of every honest wight.
Be quick in expedition, lest the sores
Of these weak Patients break into new gores.   [*Ex*. Priest.

Per. My dear, dear *Amoret*, how happy are
Those blessed pairs, in whom a little jar
Hath bred an everlasting love, too strong
For time, or steel, or envy to do wrong?
How do you feel your hurts? Alas poor heart,
How much I was abus'd; give me the smart
For it is justly mine.

Amo. I do believe.
It is enough dear friend, leave off to grieve,
And let us once more in despight of ill
Give hands and hearts again.

Per. With better will
Than e're I went to find in hottest day
Cool Crystal of the Fountain, to allay
My eager thirst: may this band never break.
Hear us O Heaven.

Amo. Be constant.

Per. Else *Pan* wreak,

With [d]ouble vengeance, my disloyalty;
Let me not dare to know the company
Of men, or any more behold those eyes.

Amo. Thus Shepherd with a kiss all envy dyes.

Enter Priest.

Priest. Bright Maid, I have perform'd your will, the Swain
In whom such heat and black rebellions raign
Hath undergone your sentence, and disgrace:
Only the Maid I have reserv'd, whose face
Shews much amendment, many a tear doth fall
In sorrow of her fault, great fair recal
Your heavy doom, in hope of better daies,
Which I dare promise; once again upraise
Her heavy Spirit that near drowned lyes
In self consuming care that never dyes.

Clor. I am content to pardon, call her in;
The Air grows cool again, and doth begin
To purge it self, how bright the day doth show
After this stormy Cloud! go *Satyr*, go,
And with this Taper boldly try her hand,
If she be pure and good, and firmly stand
To be so still, we have perform'd a work
Worthy the Gods themselves.   [*Satyr brings* Amaryllis *in.*

Satyr. Come forward Maiden, do not lurk
Nor hide your face with grief and shame,
Now or never get a name
That may raise thee, and recure
All thy life that was impure:
Hold your hand unto the flame,
If thou beest a perfect dame,
Or hast truely vow'd to mend,
This pale fire will be thy friend.
See the Taper hurts her not.
Go thy wayes, let never spot
Henceforth seize upon thy blood.
Thank the Gods and still be good.

The Faithful Shepherdess

Clor. Young Shepherdess now ye are brought again
To Virgin state, be so, and so remain
To thy last day, unless the faithful love
Of some good Shepherd force thee to remove;
Th[e]n labour to be true to him, and live
As such a one, that ever strives to give
A blessed memory to after time.
Be famous for your good, not for your crime.
Now holy man, I offer up again
These patients full of health, and free from pain:
Keep them from after ills, be ever near
Unto their actions, teach them how to clear
The tedious way they pass through, from suspect,
Keep them from wronging others, or neglect
Of duty in themselves, correct the bloud
With thrifty bits and labour, let the floud,
Or the next neighbouring spring give remedy
To greedy thirst, and travel not the tree
That hangs with wanton clusters, [let] not wine,
Unless in sacrifice, or rites divine,
Be ever known of Shepherd, have a care
Thou man of holy life. Now do not spare
Their faults through much remissness, nor forget
To cherish him, whose many pains and swet
Hath giv'n increase, and added to the downs.
Sort all your Shepherds from the lazy clowns
That feed their Heifers in the budded Brooms:
Teach the young Maidens strictness, that the grooms
May ever fear to tempt their blowing youth;
Banish all complements, but single truth
From every tongue, and every Shepherds heart,
Let them still use perswading, but no Art:
Thus holy *Priest*, I wish to thee and these,
All the best goods and comforts that may please.

Alex. And all those blessings Heaven did ever give,
We pray upon this Bower may ever live.

Priest. Kneel every Shepherd, whilest with powerful hand
I bless your after labours, and the Land
You feed your flocks upon. Great *Pan* defend you
From misfortune, and amend you,
Keep you from those dangers still,

That are followed by your will,
Give ye means to know at length
All your riches, all your strength,
Cannot keep your foot from falling
To lewd lust, that still is calling
At your Cottage, till his power
Bring again that golden hour
Of peace and rest to every soul.
May his care of you controul
All diseases, sores or pain
That in after time may raign
Either in your flocks or you,
Give ye all affections new,
New desires, and tempers new,
That ye may be ever true.
Now rise and go, and as ye pass away
Sing to the God of Sheep, that happy lay,
That honest *Dorus* taught ye, *Dorus*, he
That was the soul and god of melodie.

The SONG.   [*They all Sing*

All ye woods, and trees and bowers,
All you vertues and ye powers
That inhabit in the lakes,
In the pleasant springs or brakes,
  Move your feet
  To our sound,
  Whilest we greet
  All this ground,
With his honour and his name
That defends our flocks from blame.

He is great, and he is Just,
He is ever good, and must
Thus be honour'd: Daffodillies,
Roses, Pinks, and loved Lillies,
  Let us fling,
  Whilest we sing,
  Ever holy,
  Ever holy,
Ever honoured ever young,
Thus great Pan *is ever sung.*   [*Exeunt.*

Satyr. Thou divinest, fairest, brightest,
Thou m[o]st powerful Maid, and whitest,
Thou most vertuous and most blessed,
Eyes of stars, and golden tressed
Like *Apollo*, tell me sweetest
What new service now is meetest
For the *Satyr*? shall I stray
In the middle Air, and stay
The sayling Rack, or nimbly take
Hold by the Moon, and gently make
Sute to the pale Queen of night
For a beam to give thee light?
Shall I dive into the Sea,
And bring thee Coral, making way
Through the rising waves that fall
In snowie fleeces; dearest, shall
I catch the wanton Fawns, or Flyes,
Whose woven wings the Summer dyes
Of many colours? get thee fruit?
Or steal from Heaven old *Orpheus* Lute?
All these I'le venture for, and more,
To do her service all these woods adore.

Clor. No other service, *Satyr*, but thy watch
About these thickets, lest harmless people catch
Mischief or sad mischance.

Satyr. Holy Virgin, I will dance
Round about these woods as quick
As the breaking light, and prick
Down the Lawns, and down the vails
Faster than the Wind-mill sails.
So I take my leave, and pray
All the comforts of the day,
Such as *Phoebus* heat doth send
On the earth, may still befriend
Thee, and this arbour.

Clo. And to thee,
All thy Masters love be free.   [*Exeunt.*